Working the MISSISSIPPI

Working the MISSISSIPPI

Two Centuries of Life on the River

Bonnie Stepenoff

UNIVERSITY OF MISSOURI PRESS
COLUMBIA

University of Missouri Press, Columbia, Missouri 65201
Printed and bound in the United States of America

5 4 3 2 1 19 18 17 16 15

ISBN: 978-0-8262-2053-0
Library of Congress Control Number: 2015940296

♾™ This paper meets the requirements of the
American National Standard for Permanence of Paper
for Printed Library Materials, Z39.48, 1984.

Interior design and composition: K. Lee Design & Graphics
Typefaces: Minion and Walbaum Buch

For Syd and Lola

Contents

List of Illustrations

Acknowledgments

I owe the greatest debt of gratitude to Sean Visintainer, librarian, of the St. Louis Mercantile Library at the University of Missouri–St. Louis. He responded to numerous e-mails, guided me to books and articles, and gave me access to collections of source material on riverboats and the people who worked on them. My quest for information also took me to the St. Louis branch of the Missouri State Archives with its extensive collection of court records. Pat Barge and Michael Everman drew my attention beyond the records to books and articles that helped in my research. I found many books of interest in Kent Library at Southeast Missouri State University in Cape Girardeau. Librarians there helped me to obtain titles through interlibrary loan. I am also thankful for my connection to the Cape River Heritage Museum in Cape Girardeau, which houses a large number of photographs, books, and artifacts relating to steamboating on the Mississippi.

Several people were kind enough to sit down with me and share their memories of life on the Mississippi. Larry Drum of Cape Girardeau spoke vividly about the work of a towboat captain. Rose Marie Thrower of Cape Girardeau talked about her work as a cook on towboats. Carl Okenfuss, Don Bader, and Don Karl of Ste. Genevieve shared thoughts about their work for the U.S. Army Corps of Engineers.

Many thanks are due to Clair Willcox, Editor-in-chief; Sara Davis, Managing Editor; and the staff of the University of Missouri Press for bringing their expertise and support to this project and many other projects that have explored, illuminated, and celebrated the culture and landscape of the Mississippi River valley. It has been a privilege to work with them.

I have been lucky enough to spend the past twenty years living on the west bank of the Mississippi River. During my career I have had the opportunity to visit many libraries and historic sites in the Mississippi valley. Through this long association, I have learned to appreciate the river and its history. I have also had the good fortune to share my life with my husband, Jerry, my children and grandchildren.

Author's Note

I live in a town on the west bank of the Mississippi River. Every day, if I have the time, I can walk down the hill to the foot of Broadway, cross the railroad tracks, pass through the floodgate—unless it is closed—and come close enough to the river to hear the sound it makes. It is a surprisingly soft sound for such a big river.

That softness can fool you. When the floodgates close, you know the high water behind the fifty-foot concrete and steel wall moves with the force of an avalanche. Anyone who has lived near the river for very long has seen what a flood can do to fields, roads, cars, city streets, businesses, homes, animals, and people. But we stay anyway, or we come back, and we rebuild. There is something about the river that draws us to it and keeps us.

From St. Louis, Missouri, to Memphis, Tennessee, the river is deep, fast-moving, muddy, and wide. The Missouri River flows into it at St. Louis, adding power to its current and changing its color from blue to an earthy brown. The Mississippi is prettier above St. Louis. People go sailing and skiing on the river's tranquil surface. From St. Louis on down to Memphis, it's all, or almost all, business, unless you take pleasure in sitting on the banks and watching the barges go by. On any fine day when I go down to the waterfront, I meet old people and young people doing just that.

For some of us, the river is a connection to history. Mark Twain rode the current past my town, Cape Girardeau, and said it made "a handsome appearance." For others, the river means music. When we sit there and listen, we hear not only the sough of the water but also the ghostly piping of steam whistles and calliopes on old-time riverboats. Some of us feel awed and oddly comforted by the idea that the river was there long before we came down to see it and will be there long after we're gone, and some of us wonder what it would be like to be "out there," steering a boat through treacherous water on a night when no starlight penetrates the fog.

Introduction

There is an important difference between boating on a river and sailing on the sea: riverboats, even on the wide Mississippi, are never far from land. Even in the dark, river boatmen can smell the plants and hear the animals and the people on the banks and the wharves. In the nineteenth century, without the help of radar, Mississippi steamboat pilots navigated at night by the shadows of overhanging trees, the hum of life on the docks, and the barking of dogs. This book is about the men and women who worked on the riverboats, and it is also about the men and women who worked in boatyards, ferry landings, grocery and supply stores, and gambling dens in cities and towns along the way.[1]

In *Life on the Mississippi,* Mark Twain expressed a pilot's as well as a writer's awareness of towns that lined the riverbank. As a young man he worked on the steamboats, and as a mature and successful writer he revisited the places he remembered. Among these was the city of St. Louis, where coal smoke made even new buildings look old. There was quaint old Ste. Genevieve, a relic of French settlement in the Mississippi valley. In Twain's time, Chester entered the modern era with a railroad and a prison. Cape Girardeau, he wrote, made a "handsome appearance" with its college on top of a hill. Cairo sat brisk and bustling at the confluence of the Mississippi and Ohio rivers. New Madrid was ringed by forests, and Memphis was "nobly situated" on a lofty bluff.[2]

Before the steamboat era, flatboats and keelboats plied the waters, bringing goods and entertainment to frontier settlements. Pioneer neighbors could easily join together to build a raftlike flatboat of planks set on heavy timbers to carry their produce down the river. They usually did this in fall or early spring when the water was high and boats could float with the current. Sometimes a boatman used a pole to steer away from trouble, and sometimes the builders added small, square sails to the boat. Flatboats could travel only downstream, so the flatboatmen had to make their way home by land or find places on a keelboat. Keelboats were larger vessels, powered by oarsmen with the assistance of a small sail. The captain, or steersman, maneuvered the boat with a long oar at the stern, and the boat could travel up- or downstream.[3]

Flatboats and keelboats connected isolated settlements, towns, and cities on the east and west banks of the river. Trading boats flying calico flags would respond to hails from customers on the landings. Covered cabins and cargo boxes on keelboats contained shelves loaded with groceries, liquor, dry goods, and hardware. Tinsmiths, toolmakers, and blacksmiths traveled up and down the river, hauling the tools of their trade, and offering their services to farmers in the bottomlands. Millers fitted up boats with machines for grinding corn. Some boats traveled with libraries, museum exhibits, and theater troupes, bringing culture to frontier towns and hamlets.[4]

Crews on flatboats and keelboats struggled against rough waters and unpredictable weather. They seldom had a pilot with great knowledge of the river and its dangers. Maneuvering a crudely built and unresponsive flatboat around snags and other obstacles required luck, skill, and raw courage. Powering a loaded keelboat against the current demanded force and determination. Crews tried to keep to the slower currents near the shore. If the water was shallow and the bottom was firm, they poled the boat. When this proved impossible, they cordelled (pulled it with towropes, or cordelles). With favorable winds, they could rely on a sail, but in any case the going was very slow. Propelling a boat upstream required twice as many men and three or four times as much time as floating the same distance downstream. Boatmen had to be away from their families for months at a time.[5]

Steam power changed life on the boats and in the river towns. An early effort to operate a steamboat on the Mississippi failed in 1803. The New Madrid Earthquake of 1811 played havoc with the river, but by 1812, steamboats had begun to make regular journeys on the lower reaches of the Mississippi between Natchez and New Orleans. The first steam-powered boat to ascend the river above the mouth of the Ohio was called the *Zebulon Pike*. Crowds cheered its arrival at the foot of Market Street in St. Louis on August 2, 1817, welcoming a new era to the middle Mississippi valley. Keelboats had disappeared from the river by 1820, although flatboats continued operating on the river until the middle of the nineteenth century, when steamboating reached its peak.[6]

In the mid-nineteenth century a solid mile of steamboats lined up side by side on the St. Louis levee, and twenty of them passed Cairo every summer's day. These tall wooden boats with churning wheels, tall smokestacks, and shrill whistles carried freight and passengers to and from bustling cities and sleepy backwoods landings. Luxury boats offered sleeping and dining accommodations and entertainment. At every stop along the way, these "floating palaces" brought music, theater, and dancing to the people of the towns. The Civil War severely disrupted river traffic, and by the late 1860s, the golden age of steamboating had passed. Railroads lured away passengers and competed for freight business. In the twentieth century, diesel-powered towboats (or push-boats) and barges (resembling overgrown flatboats) took over the job of hauling freight, while a dwindling number of old-fashioned paddle-wheelers continued to ply the river, catering at last to nostalgic tourists. But for a few romantic decades, steamboats reigned as the queens of the Mississippi.[7]

The number of boats on the Mississippi did not decline even after passenger service faded away. In the 1850s twenty packet boats passed Cairo on a typical summer day, and in the 1960s an even greater number of towboats glided by the town's riverfront. These diesel-powered towboats pushed barges loaded with cars, metal girders, oil, grain, and other bulk cargo. A single barge could carry the same load as three or four steamboats, and a single towboat could push fifty times as much weight as the largest steamboat could haul. The biggest towboats could push as many as seventy-two barges. Towboats and barges generally did not carry passengers. Crews on the towboats were smaller than those on the steamboats, but they kept up many traditions of river life.[8]

Crews on steamboats and towboats ranged in number from as few as four to more than one hundred, but averaged twenty-one workers. Historian Louis Hunter has pointed out that the structure of the workforce incorporated the maritime tradition of an all-powerful captain as well as the typical industrial arrangement of skilled supervisors and unskilled labor. At the top of the hierarchy were the captain and other officers, including the engineer, who managed the boat's machinery, the pilot, who navigated, and the mate, who supervised the cabin and deck crews. If the boat carried passengers, there would be a cabin crew similar to a hotel staff of stewards, cooks, waiters, cabin boys and chambermaids. Every riverboat had a cadre of deckhands, who cleaned, fetched and carried, and kept watch, and roustabouts, who loaded and unloaded cargo.[9]

Race, nationality, and gender helped to determine a crew member's place in the hierarchy. Irish Americans and German Americans were often the boat owners and officers. Cabin boys, many of whom were also Irish American or German American, hired on to do various jobs like scouring pans, emptying wash basins, and filling water barrels. Some of these boys were runaways, and some were orphans. Recent European immigrants and African Americans could obtain work as deckhands and roustabouts. Many of the cabin workers, stewards, cooks, waiters, porters, and maids were African American, although some were white. Before the Civil War, slaves worked on many of the boats along with free blacks, native whites, and immigrants. Long after the war ended, sleeping quarters and sometimes working areas were racially segregated, especially on the larger boats. Women represented a small minority of workers, and primarily served as cooks and maids, even in the twentieth century.[10]

While there were many variations based on the type and size of boat and the character of the officers, most historians agree that crew members endured difficult and dangerous conditions. John Habermehl pointed out that employment was seasonal and often irregular; ice clogged the river in winter, and low water slowed traffic in summer. Deck crews worked night and day for a few months and then found themselves stranded in strange towns. On many boats in the nineteenth century, crew members had no beds to sleep in but had to find places among the machinery and cargo. Thomas Buchanan, writing about African American crew members, stated that the facts of life on the steamboats included severe discipline pierced by episodes of fighting, drinking, gambling, and disease. Conditions improved in the twentieth century, but life on the river always had its perils.[11]

Steamboats also posed threats to the towns along the riverbanks. In addition to depositing rough and desperate men on the wharves, the boats were sometimes a source of contagion. There is strong evidence that the 1849 outbreak of cholera originated in New Orleans and traveled upstream on riverboats. Of the first one hundred people who fell ill in St. Louis in January 1849, the majority disembarked from steamers. By the time the epidemic ran its course, more than 4,500 people had died in a city whose total population was less than 65,000. A calamity of even greater proportions, the yellow fever epidemic in Memphis in 1878 resulted in 5,000 deaths in a population of 40,000 people. The mosquito-borne virus that caused the disease thrived in humid, unsanitary conditions and was spread by victims who traveled from one place to another on crowded boats. Mrs. Kate Bionda, the first person to die in the Memphis epidemic, owned a snack shop that catered to boatmen.[12]

The complex interactions, for good or ill, between workers on the boats and workers in the riverfront cities and towns on the middle Mississippi between St. Louis and Memphis are the subject of this book. In these pages, the term *workers* includes not only laborers but also managers, business owners, opportunists, artists, gamblers, and musicians. The term *middle Mississippi* indicates a particular stretch of river that differs from the blue and glassy upper Mississippi and also differs from the broad wide band of water that rolls through the delta to New Orleans. Along the rough, muddy waterway between the great cities of St. Louis and Memphis lie dozens of small towns and river landings, but five of them serve to acquaint the reader with the drama and diversity of river life.

Chapters are arranged to give the reader a trip down the river beginning at St. Louis and an understanding of riverboat workers starting with the captains. We begin with sketches of the transformation of St. Louis from frontier landing to bustling city that grew out and away from the river. As rail lines allowed the city to expand, the riverfront declined into a desolate conglomeration of warehouses, stores, boardinghouses, brothels, and gambling dens peopled by lonely wanderers, and an old riverboat captain spending his last years among the anchors, ropes, and nautical supplies in a boat store, reminiscing with customers and friends.

Riverboat captains are worthy of special attention. They were and are a fascinating group of men. No two of them are alike, of course, but in general, they have to possess some business acumen, an ability to command respect from the crew, and the courage to deal with floods, ice, explosions, and disasters as simple facts of everyday life. Many of them found it hard to leave the river.

Early in their history, the residents of Ste. Genevieve retreated from the river. In the 1750s, the first settlers built their houses on the banks of the Mississippi and used *bateaux* (small wooden vessels) to carry furs and other trade goods. After a big flood in 1785, the *habitants* moved their houses, church, and cemetery to higher ground, but they kept farming the rich bottomland of *le grand champ* (big field). During steamboating's heyday, the water near the secluded town bristled with fallen trees and branches that snagged numerous vessels. Pilots had to memorize all the twists and turns of the river and the locations of dangerous impediments.

In the twentieth century, men from Ste. Genevieve worked on boats that cleared away snags and engaged in flood control. Despite their efforts, the town of Ste. Genevieve did not escape the river's treachery. The great flood of 1993 surged more than a mile across the river bottoms, and water filled some of the old French houses up to the eaves. The river in the vicinity of Ste. Genevieve constantly posed a challenge to pilots.

Daring and rowdy men (and women) have always found their way to the Mississippi valley, and some of them have landed in the state prison at Chester. Like other people on the riverfront, the inmates worked hard, digging limestone from quarries, breaking up rocks with sledgehammers, or working on the prison farm. The river flowing by them served as both a reminder of their confinement and a possible avenue to freedom. In many ways, these prisoners were similar to the men and women who flocked to the levees and wharves seeking employment on the boats. Roustabouts and deckhands had a reputation for drinking, brawling, and engaging in sexual encounters with women at every landing. Mates were notoriously tough and profane, sometimes cruel, and often harsh in their treatment of unruly men. But these were stereotypes. Riverboat crew members came from every walk of life. They might be young men looking for a brief period of adventure or hardened and desperate men trying to survive. Mates had to turn these diverse individuals into members of an effective workforce.

Like Napoleon's armies, riverboat crews traveled on their stomachs. Captains and mates knew that a good cook was the key to keeping a pilot happy and a crew from mutiny. Grocers and suppliers in towns like Cape Girardeau helped keep river traffic moving. One particular grocer, who was in business for many years, earned the nickname "Ace of Diamonds" from riverboat crews. People signed on to the boats as cooks, stewards, waiters, and maids for a variety of reasons. In some cases, they could make more money on the water than on land, and some people craved adventure. An exploration of the lives of stewards, cooks, and maids will show that life on the boats could be difficult and lonely. It was hard to leave family and friends for a month at a time. But river life had its consolations. A good cook enjoyed royal treatment from passengers and crew. Cooks as well as captains loved the sounds of whistles and bells, the hum of the engines, the ever-changing scenery, the unimpeded views of sunrises and sunsets, and the constant sense of movement.

All river towns benefitted economically from riverboat traffic, and all of them suffered from drainage problems and the constant threat of floods. The city of Cairo, positioned at the confluence of the Mississippi and Ohio rivers, suffered more than most. Engineers kept the boats running and also tried to control the vagaries of the intractable river. Beginning in 1817, the federal government supported a series of engineering expeditions to study western waterways, including the Ohio and Mississippi. In the 1820s Congress started appropriating money for river improvements, including the removal of snags and rocks. Federal involvement increased throughout the nineteenth and twentieth centuries, when the United States Army Corps of Engineers (Corps) transformed the Mississippi by deepening channels, improving banks and wharves, and building levees. All this massive effort improved navigation but failed to solve Cairo's problems, and the city failed to thrive.[13]

After the epic flood of 1927, the Corps proposed an enormous system of levees and floodways throughout the Mississippi valley. As a part of this plan, the Corps created the Bird's Point–New Madrid Floodway, encompassing 131,000 acres of Missouri farmland directly across the river from Cairo (from Bird's Point in northern Mississippi County to the city of New Madrid in New Madrid County, thirty-five miles to the south). To create this floodway, the Corps lowered the main levee and constructed a setback levee farther away from the river. In the event of another great flood, the Corps retained the right to deliberately breach the main levee near Bird's Point, allowing the water to flow through the floodway and reenter the Mississippi River just north of New Madrid. A sketch of life in this town, whose name is forever associated with the earthquake of 1811, will also show readers how it became the center of controversy during floods in 1937 and again in 2011, when the Corps breached the levee and deliberately flooded a huge tract of land.[14]

Natural disasters loomed over the river, but humans added their own twists to the darker aspects of river life. During steamboating's heyday, St. Louis, Cairo, and Memphis were full of brothels and gambling halls. No discussion of river life would be complete without a glimpse of the shady culture of confidence men and riverboat gamblers. Professional gamblers traveled throughout the Mississippi valley, preying upon travelers with money in their pockets and time on their hands. The riverboat gambler became a stock character in American fiction and films, and he had a basis in fact. In the twentieth century, the boats that continued to operate on the river cleaned out the gamblers, and cities like St. Louis and Memphis found other ways to prosper, although Cairo suffered from its unfortunate dependence on a shadow economy of gambling and vice.

Possibly the riverboats' and river towns' greatest contribution to American culture has been their influence on music. Memphis, in particular, was the cradle of the blues. From the very beginning, steamboats carried musicians and entertainers, spreading their cultural influence up and down the river, bringing drama and song to the towns along the way. In the twentieth century, when the steamboats' passenger and freight business declined, enterprising captains focused on short excursions featuring troupes of actors and excellent dance bands. Some performers and musicians went on to national fame through recordings, movies, and television. Others spent their lives on the river, where they helped to create and spread new and enduring musical forms. This river journey will conclude on a high note by emphasizing the soulful joy of life on the Mississippi.

Working the MISSISSIPPI

CHAPTER ONE

St. Louis, Missouri

The St. Louis levee near Eads Bridge
From the Collections of the St. Louis Mercantile Library
at the University of Missouri–St. Louis

I went meekly aboard a few of the boats that lay packed together like sardines at the long St. Louis wharf, and humbly inquired for the pilots, but got only the cold shoulder and short words from mates and clerks.

—Mark Twain, *Life on the Mississippi*

In the first half of the nineteenth century, St. Louis grew from a frontier trading post to a rapidly expanding river city powered by steam. In the winter and spring of 1803–1804, Meriwether Lewis and William Clark camped at Wood River, Illinois, across the Mississippi River from St. Louis, preparing their keelboat and *pirogues* for a bold expedition up the Missouri River. Two prominent French fur traders, Auguste Chouteau and his younger brother Pierre, welcomed the explorers to their St. Louis residences and assisted the explorers in many ways, even engaging some men to join their crew. Thirteen years later, the Chouteau brothers were past middle age and were retiring from their business when the *Zebulon M. Pike* landed at the foot of Market Street on August 2, 1817, introducing steamboats to St. Louis.[1]

Riverboat commerce brought an assortment of footloose young men to the city's wharves and streets. Native-born whites and immigrants worked in the loading areas, engine rooms, and on the decks. Black men, both slave and free, found employment as roustabouts, firemen, stewards, and cooks. In late April of 1836, a black man named Francis McIntosh arrived in town on the steamboat *Flora*. McIntosh, who worked as a steward, was probably inebriated on April 28, when he became involved in a confrontation on the wharf. Two white policemen, William Mull and George Hammond, tried to arrest a group of workers for disorderly conduct. McIntosh intervened, allowing the other workers to run away.[2]

The events following this riverfront confrontation led to McIntosh's gruesome death and vividly brought to light the racial tensions in the city. Mull and Hammond arrested McIntosh and led him toward the jail. When Hammond taunted the captive by telling him he would probably hang for what he had done, McIntosh pulled a knife, slashed Mull's abdomen, and stabbed Hammond in the throat. Mull survived, but Hammond died in the street. Bystanders rushed in and pushed McIntosh into the jail, where a mob gathered, dragged him out again, chained him to a tree, built a fire around him, and burned him to death. Fifteen or twenty people participated in the lynching, but a larger crowd watched. Reactions in the city were mixed. Some newspapers made excuses for the atrocity, but the *St. Louis Observer*, edited by Elijah Lovejoy, raged against it. Lovejoy later moved to Alton, Illinois, where he became a martyr to the antislavery cause.[3]

Violence and tragedy continued to plague the riverfront, as commerce continued to grow. On a single day, May 17, 1849, twenty boats burned in the great fire on the St. Louis wharves. They must have been "packed together like sardines" as young Samuel Clemens noted in the 1850s. The fire did not put a damper on river traffic. The boats kept coming, and in the streets along the river's edge, restaurants, laundries, grocery stores, brothels, and gambling houses vied to serve the needs of passengers and crew members, while boys like Clemens dreamed of becoming pilots.[4]

In addition to freight and passengers the riverboats brought cholera to St. Louis in the terrible epidemic of 1849. During the month of January, at least four different boats docked with sick passengers aboard: the *Amaranth* carried thirty; the *Aleck Scott,* forty; the *St. Paul,* twenty-six; and the *General Jessup* had many ailing, although the precise number is not known. At least ten of these passengers died of the contagious disease. There were no reported deaths in February, but in March and April, the death toll rose steadily to more than twenty per day. Frightened citizens hoped that the fire of May 17 would clear the riverfront of contagion, and for two weeks after that there was a brief respite as the number of deaths declined, but then the disease spread like a wildfire, with more than four hundred deaths occurring in the week before June 17.[5]

By August, the epidemic had subsided, leaving about 7 percent of the city's residents dead. During the crisis, St. Louis suffered the highest death rate of any city in the nation. Although it was not known at the time, cholera is caused by a bacterium (*Vibrio cholera*) that thrives in unsanitary water supplies and ineffective sewer systems. It was carried around the world by people traveling on oceans and rivers, and it seems clear, in hindsight, that St. Louis's water and food supplies became contaminated, spreading the disease. After the tragedy, St. Louis invested in water and sewer projects that made the city a healthier place. River traffic slowed for a short time, but by the 1850s travelers and immigrants had once again swelled the population.[6]

Among the worst perils of river transportation was ice, both when forming in the winter and when melting in the spring. The Mississippi River did not often freeze over completely at St. Louis, but the winter of 1855–1856 was exceptionally cold. On New Year's Day 1856, the river closed, and the ice continued to get thicker for several more weeks. Late in February, warm weather upstream caused a rise in the water while the river at St. Louis was still frozen. The ice began to move slowly and gradually gathered power, crowding vessels into one another then ripping them from their moorings, forcing them downstream, and slamming them into whatever lay in their path. The *Missouri Republican* estimated that about twenty boats sank, and many others suffered damage during the hour or so before the ice began to crumble. Grant Marsh, who later became a famous captain on the Missouri River, was a young watchman who was stranded aboard the *A. B. Chambers No. 2*, floating through the wreckage on the levee, expecting to die, until the boat came to a safe landing three miles from its original mooring.[7]

One person who profited from the perils of river travel was James B. Eads, who began his career as a steamboat clerk in 1838, when he was eighteen years old. Four years later, he invented a diving bell and went into the salvage business. The daring and ingenious Eads plied the river between St. Louis and New Orleans, searching for wrecked boats buried as much as sixty-five feet below the surface. By the 1850s, he owned a fleet of salvage vessels, and he probably understood the river, its currents, and its dangers as well as anyone.[8]

During the Civil War, when the Union Army undertook a massive assault on Confederate strongholds in the lower Mississippi valley, Eads set to work building ironclad gunboats for the U.S. War Department. He leased a boatyard known as "Emerson's Docks" in Carondelet, just south of St. Louis, after the yard's owner, Primus Emerson, went to Memphis to build ironclads for the Confederacy. One of Eads's armored vessels, the *Carondelet*, played a major part in General Ulysses S. Grant's campaign to gain control of the river. On April 4, 1862, the boat sped past Island No. Ten to join the Union Army at New Madrid, Missouri. After Island No. 10 fell, the *Carondelet* descended the river to join in the fighting at Fort Pillow and Memphis. When the war ended, Eads had won national fame as an engineer and a sizable fortune as a businessman.[9]

His greatest achievement came after the war with the design and construction of a path-breaking bridge. Before 1867, Eads had never built a bridge, but he knew the depth and shape of the river better than did any other engineer at the time. In July of that year, he presented a design for a massive structure composed of three 500-foot spans supported by stone arches resting on bedrock under the river. From bedrock to top, the bridge towered more than one hundred feet, in some places resting more than sixty feet under the water. For the workers who laid the foundations of the bridge, the job was dangerous—even fatal. In the late 1860s, little was known about the dangers of deep water and how rapid changes in pressure affected the body. Eads himself had frequently experienced illness after submerging in his diving bell, but he did not realize the cause. Of the six hundred men who worked in caissons (watertight enclosures) underwater while constructing the bridge, 119 suffered illness and 14 died. In spite of these tragedies and a series of design changes, in

1873, Eads's famous bridge opened, celebrated with parades, fanfare, and a one-hundred-gun salute.[10]

The Eads Bridge was a railroad bridge, a sign that foretold the end of the golden age of steamboating, but in the 1870s, most St. Louisans had no clear presentiment of what the future might bring. Steamboats still ruled the waters, and excitement ran high for the most famous steamboat race in history. On June 30, 1870, the race began between the massive steamer *Robert E. Lee* and its sleek, fast rival the *Natchez.* Without admitting publicly that they were running a race, the captains of the two boats left New Orleans simultaneously at 4:55 pm on Thursday, June 30. Reporters for various newspapers covered the story, and crowds began to gather in towns along the way. On Saturday night, when the *Lee* reached Cape Girardeau, spectators had built a bonfire on the landing. The *Lee* arrived in St. Louis at 11:25 am on the Fourth of July. The *Natchez* was delayed by fog but reached the finish line six hours later. In all the excitement of the great race, few people stopped to consider that railroad trains on regular schedules made the same trip in a single day.[11]

Railroad passengers took part in the jubilant celebration welcoming the *Lee* to St. Louis. On the morning of July 4, passengers traveling south on the Iron Mountain Railroad waved handkerchiefs and hats as the train, with its whistle screaming, raced along the tracks near the river and shot past the boat. Special excursion trains brought spectators to the riverbank. The men at Jefferson Barracks fired a gun in salute as the *Lee* rumbled north, with smoke surging from her chimneys. Deckhands and roustabouts sang songs of victory. Rooftops and windows of buildings facing the levee filled with people. Huge crowds gathered on the wharf. Steamboats tied up in the harbor blew their whistles and rang their bells. The *Lee* passed by at full speed, then turned around, came back, and landed at the wharf at the foot of Walnut Street. Police could not restrain people from boarding the boat to shake hands with and embrace the victorious crew. If this event signaled the end of an era, it came with a bang, not a whimper.[12]

Steamboats and railroads brought people of many races and nationalities to St. Louis, and newcomers struggled to make a living by opening businesses on shabby little by-ways scattered among the streets and alleyways on the riverfront. Ship's chandlers (suppliers) opened boat stores, stocked with chains, ropes, anchors, food, and clothing. A Chinese enclave known as Hop Alley occupied an area bounded by Walnut, Market, Seventh and Ninth streets. Most of the residents of Hop Alley were ordinary businessmen and their families, trying to survive by opening laundries, grocery stores, and restaurants. But the public, fueled by newspaper sensationalism, imagined it to be a world of opium sellers, drug-induced dreams, incense, and smoky rooms. Young men went there at midnight to buy "hop" and carry it away or lie in rattan bunks and smoke it in pipes.[13]

Throughout the nineteenth and early twentieth centuries, the St. Louis riverfront possessed a distinct, and sometimes shadowy, allure. People flocked there, looking for excitement and sometimes for trouble. In the brutally cold winter of 1899, a team of grifters conducted a shell-game on folding tables set up on the ice halfway across the river. Within a short period of time, a crowd gathered around them. Three men ran the games, while another three mingled with the crowd. The men playing the games kept three walnut shells moving at a rapid pace, while keeping up a constant line of patter. Bettors had to guess which of the shells concealed a little black ball, which most likely was hidden under the shell man's thumb. The game was rigged; the bettors always lost. But the police could do nothing to stop it, because it took place on the river, out of their jurisdiction.[14]

Local authorities consistently failed to enforce laws against gambling. On October 11, 1878, the *St. Louis Evening Post* printed a letter from a concerned citizen to the St. Louis Board of Commissioners. The writer identified seventeen keno and faro houses on Sixth Street, Chestnut Street, and Washington Avenue. He further stated that a "great number of poker rooms," too numerous to mention, operated in private homes, and he begged the commissioners to break up these games and protect the public morals. Journalists J. A. Dacus and James W. Buel confirmed that there were dozens of gambling houses on Fourth, Fifth, and Sixth streets in the vicinity of the river and that these places were open for business day and night. Occasional police raids did nothing to put a damper on illegal games.[15]

Prostitution flourished in the streets nearest the river and spread to other thoroughfares as the city expanded westward. On Sixth, Seventh, and Poplar streets and Almond Avenue, at every hour of the day and night, lewd women leaned from upstairs windows, couples standing on the sidewalks embraced, drunkards slept in doorways, and men of all ages loafed and brawled in saloons. A grand jury investigation in 1881 identified two hundred brothels in the downtown area from the levee to Twelfth Street. Later in that decade, houses of prostitution spilled over into the area west of Twelfth Street and east of Fifteenth Street along Chestnut, Market, and Pine. Despite the efforts of city officials to confine the institution to the seedier neighborhoods, as respectable residents moved west, prostitutes took up residence in gaudily furnished houses throughout the city, and madams rode in elegant horse-drawn carriages.[16]

On the dark streets near the river, violent crime also flourished. Dacus and Buel went undercover to investigate the night life on Broadway between Fourth and Ninth streets, where streetwalkers and gamblers were most numerous. Larceny, burglary, robbery, assault, and murder occurred more commonly in this area than in any other part of the city. Dacus and Buel constructed the common tale of a deckhand receiving his pay and spending the night in a boardinghouse on the levee. Observing that he had fifty or a hundred dollars in his pocket, predatory men might induce him to go drinking in one of the all-night saloons. On the following morning, his body might turn up "stiff and cold on the levee," or he might just disappear into the river. No one would investigate. "He was only a deck-hand, may be, without home or friends. None will ever know his resting place."[17]

As the streets near the river became meaner in the late nineteenth century, the city expanded to the west. Theodore Dreiser, who arrived from Chicago in 1892, worked as a newspaper reporter. He found the riverfront in a state of decline. Far from downtown, on the West End, wealthy people were building magnificent homes in gated parks. At the same time, he observed, old mansions near the central business district were falling into disrepair. Stores, factories, and offices, even a few tall Chicago-style buildings, were rising in their places. Dreiser took up residence in a seedy rooming house on Pine Street, where the streetcars clanged all night long. When he walked along the waterfront, he found a mill area flanked by "wretched tenements, as poor and grimy and dingy as any" he had seen in Chicago.[18]

On May 27, 1896, a tornado (known as the Great Cyclone) brought death and destruction to the St. Louis levee. Early that afternoon, a fitful wind came from the northwest. Just after 5:00 pm masses of clouds darkened the city, and rain began to fall. Within minutes, the tornado touched down. Lightning and wind turned telegraph poles into pillars of flame. Pedestrians ran for cover through torrents of rain, dodging flying bricks and timbers. Lafayette Park suffered severe damage. Soulard Market, the City Hospital, and the City Poor House also were centers of destruction. From Broadway to the river, much of the town lay in ruins. On the morning after the storm, masses of people searched through the wreckage or clamored outside the morgue, trying to find their loved ones. In all, the storm killed about three hundred people and injured about one thousand.[19]

A steamboat captain named Louis Rosche lost everything in the cyclone. As he recalled, he had gone into a boat store to buy some clothes, including a new coat, and some rope. When he was buttoning up his new coat, the roof caved in, and plaster rained down on his head. A falling rafter sliced an arm off another man in the store. Rosche and the bleeding man ran outdoors and looked at the river. Among the scores of boats tied up at the landing was Rosche's *J. J. O'Dill.* He stood and watched as a huge dark wave lifted it up and sent it crashing onto the Eads Bridge. The boat's boilers exploded, and wreckage flew in all directions. On the bridge overhead, the wind upset a locomotive, and its wheels spun in the air. Rosche found the bartender from his boat, alive, in a pile of splintered railroad ties. Five of his passengers had been knocked overboard and drowned. Rosche was lucky to survive, but all his money was tied up in his boat, and the insurance barely covered his debts.[20]

Captain Henry Leyhe liked to tell a story about the Great Cyclone. He was onboard the *Louis Houck*, anchored just south of the St. Louis docks, when the winds began to rise. At five minutes before five o'clock (he remembered the time to the minute), clouds came from the west, the wind whirled ferociously, and the river began to churn. Boats that were not anchored broke like twigs. "Our own boat rocked and bounced against the shore," he recalled. Everyone on the boat survived, but one of his crew members, a carpenter named John Agnew, left, swearing he would never ride the river again. He walked from the dock into the city, believing he would find safe haven, but the wind had not died down. A plank flew through the air and lodged in his neck. As soon as he was released from the hospital, he returned to the boat. "I'm here to stay," he said to Leyhe, "No more landlubbin' for me."[21]

In the early twentieth century, the riverfront was still a dangerous place. On June 6, 1905, officers arrested William Arstie, publisher of the *Waterways Journal*, for brandishing a gun at the captain and the pilot of the excursion boat *Corwin H. Spencer.* When the policemen apprehended him at the headquarters of the Pilots' Association, Arstie said that Captain

Henry Bolaski and the pilot T. Wadlington had spoken roughly to him and made threatening gestures, and so he pulled out his 38-caliber pistol. After he pointed the gun at them, Bolaski and Wadlington took refuge on the boat. Arstie further stated that crew members of the *Corwin H. Spencer* had assaulted him on a previous occasion. Police contacted the assistant district attorney, who determined that Arstie's act was justified as self-defense.[22]

City, state, and national officials tried to rejuvenate the riverfront and reinvigorate commerce on the river with a convention and steamboat parade in the fall of 1907. President Theodore Roosevelt boarded the U.S. government steamer *Mississippi* in Keokuk, Iowa, on the first day of the month and arrived in St. Louis the next day. A large fleet of steamboats converged on the city and paraded downstream as far as Jefferson Barracks. Several of the boats, including the *Alton* and the *Cape Girardeau* continued on to Memphis, the site for the convention hosted by Lakes-to-Gulf Deep Waterway Association. At a point south of St. Louis, the *Alton* blew four blasts on her whistle; the *Mississippi* stopped, and the two boats came alongside each other and were lashed together. The *Alton*'s distinguished passengers, including several state governors, served an elegant banquet in the president's honor.[23]

Businessmen and politicians continued their efforts to save the St. Louis riverfront during a period of rapid decline in the first half of the twentieth century. While the Great Depression ravaged the city, Mayor Bernard Dickmann and a group of civic-minded businessmen made ambitious plans to clean up the blighted riverfront area. In 1934, Congress established a Federal Memorial Commission to create a monument to the explorers, hunters, trappers, and pioneers who had passed through St. Louis on their way to the far West. Within a year, the city had passed a bond issue to support demolition in a forty-block area south of the Eads Bridge. Project planners saved the Old Cathedral, which dated from 1834, but destroyed warehouses and other historic buildings to clear the area that would eventually become the Jefferson National Expansion Memorial, encompassing an underground museum and the magnificent Gateway Arch.[24]

In the meantime, homeless people settled on the levee in the area south of the central business district between the railroad tracks and the river. Between 1930 and 1936, St. Louis had the nation's largest Hooverville, named for President Herbert Hoover, who failed to help people displaced by the Depression. Individuals and families built dwellings out of local stones, railroad ties, trash, and discarded pieces of wood and metal. At its peak, St. Louis's Hooverville had an estimated three thousand residents, including more than three hundred children living in six hundred makeshift homes. Soulard merchants donated produce to the squatters, and Pevely Dairy delivered milk. The "Welcome Inn" under the MacArthur Bridge served meals and functioned as a post office and city hall. But the community didn't last. It was displaced in connection with a massive land clearance and public works project that made way, in the mid-twentieth century, for the Jefferson Memorial.[25]

One remnant of the age of steamboats found a home in St. Louis in 1937, when the *Goldenrod* showboat permanently docked at the Locust Street landing. Constructed in 1909, the *Goldenrod*, measuring two hundred by forty feet, was the largest showboat ever to ply the river. The stage faced an auditorium that seated more than twelve hundred. Thousands of lights, full-length mirrors, and deep red draperies created an illusion of opulence. Small-town audiences diminished after 1910, when other forms of entertainment, including motion picture shows, became available. The *Goldenrod*'s owner, Captain J. W. "Billy" Menke, sought a more stable audience in the big city. In 1940, Menke cut a steel hull from a barge and attached it to the *Goldenrod*, making it stronger and more fireproof. By 1953, only two showboats were still in business. The *Majestic* still plied the rivers, and the *Goldenrod* remained anchored at St. Louis. Throughout the 1950s and 1960s, the *Goldenrod* specialized in old-time melodramas, evoking nostalgia for days gone by on the Mississippi.[26]

Even in its decline, the seedy St. Louis riverfront found its way into popular culture in music and lyrics that long outlived the great floating palaces. When W. C. Handy wrote the "St. Louis Blues" in 1914, he was middle-aged and successful, but he had not forgotten his early years of sleeping on the cobblestones down by the wharf, hungry, unshaven, and broke. He remembered an inebriated and broken-hearted woman, stumbling along, muttering as she walked, and he tried to capture her loneliness in his song. "St. Louis woman with all her diamond rings / She leads that man around by the apron strings / 'Tweren't for powder and for store-bought hair / That man of mine would not have gone nowhere."

The feelings expressed in the lyrics are universal, but they acquired their grittiness and their edge from a connection with a run-down, dingy levee, left dark and empty after the big lighted boats were gone.[27]

CHAPTER TWO

Captains

The *Robert E. Lee* and the *Great Republic* at Cairo
From the Collections of the St. Louis Mercantile Library
at the University of Missouri–St. Louis

Captain Andy thought only in terms of waterways. Despite the prim little house in Thebes, home, to Andy, was a boat. Towns and cities were to him mere sources of supplies and passengers, set along the river banks for the convenience of steamboats.

—Edna Ferber, *Show Boat*

Riverboat captains were the masters of their vessels. They relied on pilots to understand the twists and turns of the river, engineers to keep the machinery running, and mates to manage their crews. Captains took responsibility for the freight and passengers, earning praise or blame for the outcome of every journey. Often they owned or held a financial interest in a boat or line of boats. Successful captains tended to share some characteristics, including pride, self-confidence, courage, and an entrepreneurial spirit.

William Conley, master and commander of the steamboat *Hope*, demonstrated these qualities in his career on the river. In April 1863, a slave owner sued Conley for $1,000 in damages for unlawfully transporting a slave named Arminta from Cape Girardeau to St. Louis. William C. Ranney testified that he owned the girl, known as "Minty," who was about eighteen years old, of medium height, with a yellow complexion. A witness, John Beardslee, stated that he knew Ranney, Conley, and Minty. Beardslee said that he spoke with Conley on April 21, 1863, and the captain explained that he had brought the girl on his boat as a servant to a woman called, he believed, Mrs. White, although he was not certain of the woman's name. He asserted that he would not have allowed Minty onboard if he had known she was a runaway slave. Someone handed him a note saying that she was a fugitive, but he did not look at it until he had left the boat and gone into the city. When he took it out of his pocket and read it, he returned to the boat, but Minty was gone. The jury found for the plaintiff and made Captain Conley pay one hundred dollars.[1]

Conley was a native of Pennsylvania, a free state. Some steamboat captains supported slavery and even used slave labor. But Conley did not, and it seems very convenient that he could not remember the name of the woman who had brought Minty onboard the boat and had neglected to read the note about Minty's status until it was too late. If he did not knowingly participate in freeing the slave girl, he certainly turned a blind eye to "Mrs. White" and her activities.[2]

Like many captains, Conley was a venture capitalist, who won and lost money on several boats. Riverboats were risky enterprises. They frequently sank in dangerous rivers or burst into flames because of boiler explosions. Captain Conley, for example, invested in the stern-wheeler *Fontenelle,* which had sunk in the Missouri River in 1868 but been raised and repaired. Unfortunately, the *Fontenelle* hit another snag and sank again near St. Joseph, Missouri, in 1871. Damages to the boat and cargo reportedly amounted to more than $20,000. Potential profits must have made the risks worth taking. In 1870, Conley lived in St. Louis, where he owned real estate worth $7,000 and personal property worth $4,000.[3]

The steamboat *Hope* had a similarly checkered career. On July 24, 1863, Confederate forces burned the boat in the Yazoo River to keep her from falling into the hands of Federal forces. After the Civil War ended, the federal government raised what was left of the boat and found that the boilers, engines, and water wheels remained in good condition. The boat chugged her way to Memphis and eventually was rebuilt. In 1879, Captains August Wohlt and William L. Heckman of Hermann, Missouri, purchased the rebuilt *Hope* and used her to tow barges loaded with railroad ties for the Missouri Pacific Railroad.[4]

Because of the well-known dangers they faced, riverboat captains could cut a dashing figure and could expect some success with the ladies. According to the 1850 U.S. Census, Captain Conley lived in Bridgeport (Fayette County), Pennsylvania, with his wife, Christina, and three children. It is unclear how his marriage to Christina ended, but in 1870, according to the census of that year, he lived in St. Louis with a wife named Elizabeth and their three-year-old son. Conley was fifty-seven years old at the time, and his wife was thirty-five.[5]

Steamboat captains were the lords of multistory "palaces" that towered above the surface of mighty rivers. On the lower (main) deck, firemen stoked the boilers that generated power to turn the big wheels that rolled through the water. Among the boilers and machinery, livestock shuffled in wooden pens, freight rested heavily in barrels and crates, and deckhands found places to lay their heads for a few hours rest. Above them, on the second (cabin) deck, passengers slept, ate, played cards, listened to music, and watched the river go by. The roof over their heads formed the hurricane deck, which contained the officers' and cooks' quarters and the "texas," a small compartment where crews could smoke cigars or pipes. At the highest point on the boat, above the texas, was the pilothouse, which commanded a panoramic view of the water and the shoreline. A large vessel could carry five hundred to seven hundred tons of freight or three hundred to four hundred passengers, and the captain was responsible for the safety of them all.[6]

William "Buck" Leyhe (pronounced "lie") lived the life of a steamboat captain for more than half a century and knew what it was like to ride high above the glassy water or drag a wrecked boat out of the mud. He inherited a love for life on the river. Before he was born, his father had salvaged a wreck from the Mississippi, repaired it, and launched it as the *Young Eagle*. It was a small boat, only 84 feet long and 14 feet wide, that carried people and freight on a five-mile run from Warsaw, Illinois, to Keokuk, Iowa. His son William was born in Warsaw in 1873, but he grew up in Quincy, Illinois. William admired a fireman named "Buck," who worked on the river, and took the nickname for himself. From an early age, Buck Leyhe worked for his father, first in Quincy and later Alton,

Captain William "Buck" Leyhe
From the Collection of the Cape River Heritage Museum, Cape Girardeau

Illinois. As a young man, he relocated to St. Louis, where he and his older brother Henry took over his father's business, the Eagle Packet Company. Before his death on July 4, 1956, Captain Leyhe had become legendary for his long and eventful career.[7]

In 1903, when the captain and his brother took charge of the business, communities along the Missouri and Mississippi rivers were experiencing a great flood. Railroad lines in and out of St. Louis were under water, and the Alton Railroad arranged with the Eagle Packet Company to operate two boats a day between Alton and Chicago. Captain Leyhe took charge of the *Spread Eagle,* and for several weeks, the boat carried passengers, mail, milk, and food into St. Louis, keeping the city in touch with the outside world until the floodwaters subsided. The company received excellent publicity and substantial financial gain for its services during this emergency.[8]

In his travels on the river, Leyhe often visited Cape Girardeau, where he met and married a local woman, Mary Filburn, in 1896. The young couple lived in a house on a hill near the red brick courthouse. The captain's two dogs would come running down the hill when they heard the sound of the riverboat's whistle. Leyhe took Toodles, a male collie, to St. Louis, where he was hit by a streetcar in July 1910. The captain brought the dog's body back to Cape Girardeau on the *Spread Eagle* for burial. It seems that Leyhe's loyalties were divided. In the summer of 1913, Mary filed for divorce, claiming he was "guilty of adultery with divers persons at divers times and places" and that he had "openly and notoriously cohabited for a space of several years" with "a certain woman in the City of St. Louis, Missouri." Captain Leyhe married Emma Ponti in St. Louis in 1914. His first wife died in 1918.[9]

Leyhe, a burly man more than six feet tall and weighing more than two hundred pounds, had a way with the ladies and also with the passengers. Nothing energized him more than a boat filled with people. During a trip, he slept little and constantly made the rounds, joining card games and telling humorous stories. He especially liked one about a pilot who was told to watch out for eddies. The pilot steadied himself during the vigil with a jug of whiskey. Passing a log cabin, the pilot saw lights and heard laughter; that called for a drink. Soon enough he saw another cabin, bright with lights, and filled with happy people. He drank to that. When the captain came on deck, the pilot reported that people were holding dances all along the river. "You fool," said the captain, "we're in the eddy. We're going around in circles!"[10]

Another story he liked to tell hinted at an edgier world below the passenger deck. While captains mingled with cardplayers and revelers, mates had to keep a tight rein on the crews who handled the cargo. Many of these crew members were rough and reckless, and the mates had to be intimidating. One of the toughest of these mates, Charley Botsh, worked occasionally for Captain Leyhe. According to the captain, Botsh had an effective way of quelling any disturbances among the crew. He would ask one of the men to set up a kernel of corn, and he would shoot it off its perch with his revolver. That usually put an end to any trouble with the crew.[11]

Captain Leyhe himself showed the dark side of his nature when faced with rebellious crew members. On July 16, 1907, the roustabouts who loaded and unloaded the *Grey Eagle* complained about their wages. At the time, the vessel was docked at the St. Louis wharf. The roustabouts' spokesman, a man known as Priest Dedman, or "Crying John," got into an argument with second mate Joseph Langevin. Langevin struck Dedman, and Dedman retaliated. First mate William McClatchey and Captain Leyhe intervened, and the violence escalated.[12]

The details of what happened remain unknown, but during the struggle, Dedman went overboard, was pulled under by the current, and did not surface. Police arrived on the scene and took the first and second mates into custody as a menacing crowd gathered. Later, the police questioned Captain Leyhe, who stated that he did not know how Dedman went overboard. Leyhe appeared before a judge, who released him on bail and ordered him to appear in St. Louis Circuit Court in October. Ten days after the fight, Dedman's body was found downriver.[13]

No charges appear to have been filed against Leyhe or the Eagle Packet Company in connection with Dedman's death. The captain's name does not appear in circuit court records from 1907 to 1911. Prosecutors apparently concluded that there was not enough evidence to warrant bringing the case to trial. Was Leyhe capable of throwing a man overboard? There is no way to answer conclusively. Employees of the company and associates of Captain Leyhe have stated that he was a moody man who could take swift and harsh action against employees who crossed him. He had his good and bad sides, and he was tough enough to thrive in the risky and turbulent world of the river.[14]

As master and commander, Leyhe lost his share of boats. On July 10, 1910, a steamer named *Cape Girardeau* hit a snag at Turkey Island (near Chester, Illinois) and sank. The captain guided all the passengers to safety, but the boat was a total loss. Six years later, the second boat named *Cape Girardeau* sank, and once again the captain rescued all the people onboard. But he lost a very valuable cargo and went to great lengths to salvage what he could. On October 18, three days after the wreck, the Eagle Packet Company sent barges and divers to remove as much cargo as possible from the submerged vessel. Once the divers had brought up what they could, they dynamited the wreckage to break up the deck and allow boxes and barrels of merchandise to float to the surface. According to court documents, the boat was carrying $48,000 worth of goods, and the company had only $35,000 in insurance coverage.[15]

In the aftermath of this wreck, Leyhe went hunting through the streets of St. Louis for hundreds of feet of kid leather, which he claimed had floated up out of the boat and been stolen. The leather had been intended for the International Shoe Company's factory in Cape Girardeau. Leyhe alleged that small shoe manufacturers in St. Louis had somehow recovered pieces of the leather and taken it to their shops. The Eagle Packet Company sued a man named Louis Boulton, claiming that he had $575 worth of stolen leather in his shop at 1718 Franklin Avenue. The company filed a similar case against G. Z. Davis for recovery of forty-eight pieces of black calf leather worth $240.00 from his shop at the corner of Sixteenth and Washington. The actions were unsuccessful, but the incident illustrates the value of the cargoes on Mississippi riverboats and the determination of captains to collect what they believed was due them.[16]

Sometimes a captain's best efforts to preserve his boats and their cargo failed. In 1918, the Leyhe brothers sent most of their fleet ten miles up the Tennessee River for winter mooring. The Tennessee generally did not freeze, but in the winter of 1917–1918, the ice was nine inches thick. Late in January 1918, warm rains in the Tennessee valley caused a flood that washed the ice along with *Alton, Peoria, Grey Eagle*, and *Spread Eagle* out of the river. In the same disaster, the Eagle Packet Company lost a tug boat, a work boat, a wharf boat, and two coal barges. The loss amounted to half a million dollars, only a tenth of which was covered by insurance. The company had only the *Bald Eagle*, the *Piasa*, and a wharf boat in St. Louis. In the wake of this calamity, the Leyhes bought the *William Garig*, which they rebuilt and renamed the *Golden Eagle*.[17]

In the 1920s and early 1930s, Captain Leyhe commanded another boat named after the city of Cape Girardeau (the third boat with that name). The people of that small city had a steadfast attachment to the captain, and the local chamber of commerce had offered to help him when he suffered his great losses in 1918. For many years, the city's residents had depended on Leyhe's boats for freight and passenger service and also for entertainment. The third steamer *Cape Girardeau* had previously operated under several other names. On April 23, 1924, at a special christening ceremony, giving the boat its new name, city leaders presented the captain

The steamboat *Cape Girardeau*
From the Collection of the Cape River Heritage Museum, Cape Girardeau

with a bronze plaque in recognition of his many years of service. The *Cape Girardeau* almost always carried an orchestra, which would entertain residents who came down to the dock. On March 27, 1926, onboard the *Cape Girardeau*, the captain entertained the famous evangelist Billy Sunday at dinner. Later in his life, Captain Leyhe recalled, "In those days the whole population would turn out when a boat made for shore. Yes, we were some shucks. The whole town celebrated; dances, free drinks once around.... Ah, yes."[18]

The glory days of passenger service on the river had ended by 1935; the company sold the *Cape Girardeau*, and Captain Leyhe took command of the *Golden Eagle*. The captain, who was sixty-two years old and also past his prime, was not yet ready to give up his life on the river. On April 22, 1939, he accepted a challenge to race against the *Delta Queen*, a California steamer. The boats ran the race on separate rivers: the *Golden Eagle* on the Mississippi and the *Delta Queen* on the Sacramento, and the *Golden Eagle* beat the newer boat's time. On June 1, 1941, the *Golden Eagle* hit a submerged dike near Chester, Illinois. All the passengers escaped, but the boat was wrecked. Captain Leyhe struggled to refurbish it, but he could not obtain a new boiler until after World War II. The boat did not run again until 1946. On May 17, 1947, the seventy-four-year-old Leyhe was onboard as a passenger when the *Golden Eagle* ran aground at Grand Tower, eighty miles north of Cairo, and went down for the last time.[19]

The aging captain still clung to his life on the river. In the 1950s, he was president of the firm, with his two sons, Fred and William Jr., acting as general manager and vice president, respectively. An important part of the family enterprise was the Eagle Boat Store, a cavernous warehouse full of iron and steel chains, huge coils of rope, and marine hardware, including 2000-pound anchors. When he gave up riding on the boats, Captain Leyhe spent a great deal of time in the store, which provided passing boats with groceries, supplies, equipment, and all manner of nautical items. Old crew members served the customers, while the captain sat at a rolltop desk answering letters and passing the time of day with friends and acquaintances. When a local reporter visited the store in 1951, the captain told him that business was flourishing. Passenger boats had all but disappeared from the river, but there was more freight trade than ever before. He advised ambitious young men to sign on as deckhands and study for pilots' licenses. The work was interesting, and the pay was good.[20]

As an old man, Leyhe reflected on the danger and beauty of the river. "Directly beneath the window of my office at the Eagle Boat Store," he wrote, "swirls the water of the Mississippi, seven feet deep at the building line." When he wrote these words in 1947, St. Louis had experienced a disastrous flood, but Leyhe reminded residents "what a blessing the great stream is. She carried a monumental amount of our commerce—and still does. She has transported her passengers. She lends fertility to the land." People who lived near the river knew that. The difference between river folk and the rest of humanity, he said, "is the philosophical way many of us close to the river take a flood. You might say we take the high water as it comes."[21]

Leyhe's admirers saw in him a man who did just that: he took the high water as it came. Every year during the late 1940s and early 1950s, the Golden Eagle Club held a banquet in the captain's honor, although he was often too ill to attend. In July 1956, he suffered a heart attack and was taken to Barnes Hospital in St. Louis. Local radio stations broadcast frequent updates on his condition. He was released on July 2, but on July 4, the eighty-three-year-old Leyhe returned to the hospital after suffering a hemorrhage. His two sons and their wives sat with him throughout the day until he passed away at ten o'clock that night. His wife, the former Emma Ponti, had passed away in 1945. An editorial in the *St. Louis Post-Dispatch* paid tribute to Leyhe, saying that "he knew what it was to be wrecked and to have a boat go down in the very waters that had floated him minutes before."[22]

Leyhe was right about one thing. Freight traffic flourished on the Mississippi long after passenger service faded, and young men could still have careers on the river. One man who started as a deckhand, earned a pilot's license, and eventually became a captain was Larry Drum of Cape Girardeau. Why did he do it? "Well," he said in an interview, "it was family. My dad worked out there." He used the phrase "out there" to mean on the river. "I had a lot of friends. I got out of school, and instead of going to college I went out there." He worked as a deckhand for six years, and Captain Louis Owens took an interest in him.[23]

Owens encouraged Drum to become a pilot. "He put me in the pilot house as a steersman," Drum said. The captain made him draw maps of the river. "Every time I steered a section of river I redid my maps, put in all the dikes and buoys." By the time Drum worked in the pilothouse, the Corps had improved the navigability and safety of the river by dredging the channel, building levees and dikes, and installing buoys and lights. The federal government regulated workers on the river. "You had to have a license from the Coast Guard to be a pilot," Drum said. "There was a test with a hundred questions, and you had to draw [maps of] the river to get a license." This was in the 1960s. "Then later we had to do radar training."[24]

After working as a pilot for sixteen years, Drum spent twenty years as a captain on towboats. "All that is," he commented, "is a glorified pilot that takes care of everything." A captain on the river, he remarked, was not like a sea captain. "It's not like salt water. Now a salt water captain is god." During his twenty years as a captain, conditions changed. In the beginning, he said, the captain hired his own crew, but as time went on, administrators took over. "They've got a management team that does the hiring and firing and whatever," including the procurement of fuel and food. "The captain's power and status eroded."[25]

During his long career, Drum served on 120 different towboats, which pushed, rather than towed, barges loaded with freight. He had a regular job with Archer-Daniels-Midland, but on his days off he would work for other companies. His regular schedule was thirty days on and thirty days off. The boats he rode pushed barges loaded with anything and everything from televisions to motorcycles to cooking oil. There was no regular passenger service, but sometimes there would be guests onboard—dignitaries, stockholders, family and friends of crew members.[26]

Mostly, he traveled with a ten-man crew: nine men and one woman, who was the cook. Early in his career, the boats would have a maid, who took care of the upstairs quarters for the captain, the chief engineer, and the assistant engineer. The maid cleaned the bedrooms, made the beds, and helped the cook. In later years, the cook had modern conveniences, including an electric dishwasher, and there was no longer a maid. Deckhands took care of the main (lower) deck. The mate supervised the deck crew, and the chief engineer took care of the engine room. The engineer had his own crew. If anything happened to the captain, the engineer took charge; the pilot did the steering and ranked third in command.[27]

Part of the captain's job was making sure everybody got along. Fighting and squabbling were not tolerated. "You couldn't have it in that close quarters," Drum said. As long as they were well fed, he said, the crew was generally peaceful. Crew members worked six-hour watches and then had six hours off. The captain himself stood watch from breakfast until lunch and then went up to bed. At four-thirty, he would have supper and then stand watch from six until midnight. The men in the crew followed similar schedules, with six-hour watches throughout the day and night. There was a front watch and a back watch detail.[28]

Captain Owens taught Drum to be strict with his men. "The old captain trained me," said Drum. After lunch, he did a walk-around, and if things weren't painted or cleaned up, he'd get on the mate. Then the mate got on the deck crew." In praise of a mate named Verdell Ledgewood from Iuka, Mississippi, Drum said, "He kept a clean boat." Deckhands slept two to a room, "but they were on opposite watches so there was one man in a room at a time." Some deckhands were young; for some, this was their first time away from home. The mate might have to remind the new ones to take a bath. Crew received clean sheets once a week; linens were sent to laundries in river towns. But, according to Drum, "A lot of them would just throw their linen up there and sleep on top of it, so they wouldn't have to change their bed." Deckhands shared a bath between every two rooms. The captain, the pilot, the chief engineer, and the cook each had a private bath.[29]

Drum remembered lots of the men he traveled with, including one captain he worked for named Edgar Allan Poe. "His mother liked Edgar Allan Poe stories, so she named him after him. After he retired he went to Nashville and was captain on the *General Jackson* over there at Opryland." Drum enjoyed being "out there" with good companions. Camaraderie was one of the charms of life on the river, but family life could be difficult for river men. He said, "It was going and coming that was hard, and I lost a lot of time with the boys." He had two sons. He and his wife, Joann, were married more than fifty years. "It's unusual," he said, "for a river man to stay married that long. There's a lot of divorces among river people. But it just worked out."[30]

Even in the twentieth century, after the Corps made navigation safer, there were dangers on the river. The worst things about a captain's job, said Drum, were ice and high water. Ice floes were a threat in the winter, and melting ice brought high water in the spring. "You've really got to watch that current in high water because it will cross you. It will take you sideways." Radar would show the locations of buoys and the height of the bridges. When the water was high, the crew would have to take down the antennas and the flagpole to get under the bridges. Even so, Captain Drum hit a couple of bridges in his time. Travel in the summer was less treacherous, but low water could be hazardous, too, because the boats could run aground. Once he was caught on a sandbar near Cairo. It took three days digging to free three loaded barges from the sand.[31]

For men like Conley, Leyhe, and Drum, the dangers were part of the charm of their job. The same independent streak that moved Conley to let a slave escape led him to invest and reinvest in boats and take the losses when they went down. Leyhe had three boats sink from under him, lost most of his fleet to ice and high water, and still could not leave his life on the river. Drum regretted being away from his sons as they grew up, but looked back fondly on his river career. "My first job was on an oil tow, four barges of gas, out of St. Louis. I went out as green as grass. They taught me what I needed to know. I went from deckhand to relief mate to pilot to captain. It was an interesting life. I enjoyed making a boat try to do what I wanted it to do."[32]

CHAPTER THREE

Ste. Genevieve, Missouri

Towboats at Ste. Genevieve in high water
Photograph courtesy of B. H. Rucker

> I suspected that it might be Ste. Genevieve—and so it proved to be. Observe what this eccentric river had been about: it had built up this huge, useless tow-head [island] directly in front of this town, cut off its river communications, fenced it away completely, and made a "country" town of it. It is a fine old place, too, and deserved a better fate. It was settled by the French and is a relic of a time when one could travel from the mouth of the Mississippi to Quebec and be on French territory and under French rule all the way.
>
> —Mark Twain, *Life on the Mississippi*

The French *habitants* of the old village of Ste. Genevieve moved their church, dwellings, trading posts, and cemetery farther from the river after the flood of 1785. In the 1790s, New Ste. Genevieve was a thriving little town on the banks of two pretty little streams called the North and South

Gabouri that flowed into the Mississippi. By the mid-nineteenth century, the town's population included Anglo, German, and African Americans, who farmed the flood-enriched bottomlands. As Twain noted, Ste. Genevieve had many characteristics of a "country" town, but its residents' lives remained closely connected to the boats that plied the Mississippi River.

By the time they moved their town to higher ground, the residents of Ste. Genevieve had developed a taste for luxury items from New Orleans. From the earliest days of the settlement small wooden *bateaux* carried flour, wheat, and corn upriver to St. Louis and downriver to the Gulf. A skillful *voyageur* (boatman) could maneuver a boat from Ste. Genevieve to New Orleans in three weeks, but the trip back took three months or more. Hired men and slaves used oars to power the vessels, and boats sometimes traveled in convoys. Boats returning to Ste. Genevieve brought household goods that included gunpowder, nails, cloth, shoes, stockings, blankets, soap, thread, crockery, wine, rum, sugar, and coffee. By the early nineteenth century shipments from New Orleans included expensive items like Havana cigars, fancy soaps, handkerchiefs, fans, crystal goblets, and delicate parasols. After steamboats appeared on the river, the people of this back-country town retained their connection to the fashionable world. Twain made note of this when he observed "a well-dressed lady and gentleman, and two well-dressed ladylike young girls" disembarking near a hidden town that he supposed must be Ste. Genevieve.[1]

With their long-standing ties to the river trade, quite naturally, some of the townsmen went to work on the steamboats. For example, Louis Cavelier took a job as a blacksmith on the *Mandan.* In fact, he may have been the boat's engineer, because on these early boats, the engineers used blacksmithing skills to repair machinery. Cavelier's family history is very interesting; he was a descendant of a free woman of color named Catherine Coton de Mahi, who was listed as a *comercianta* (merchant) in the Spanish census of 1787. Catherine died in 1790, and her daughter Mari entered the household of a Frenchman named Etienne Parent as a servant. She remained there until her marriage in 1799. Her husband, Louis Cavelier, served in the first Ste. Genevieve militia. The local church at that time recognized unions between men and women of different races, and several prominent Frenchmen, including Parent, served as witnesses at their wedding.[2]

Their son Louis, who was born about 1805, was one of six children. The members of the Cavelier family (sometimes recorded as the Louison family) lived as free black people in Ste. Genevieve in the decades preceding the Civil War. Young Louis Cavelier (also known as Louis Louison) apparently worked on the *Mandan* in the early 1820s. In 1822, the sheriff in Ste. Genevieve ordered the boat's owners to pay him $28.00 in wages. The *Mandan* sank near Vicksburg, Mississippi, on November 20, 1824. The records do not tell whether or not Cavelier went to work on another boat, but he continued to live in Ste. Genevieve with his wife, Mellory, (whose name may have been misspelled in the census) into the 1880s.[3]

Some of the wealthier citizens of Ste. Genevieve invested in steamboats. A group of prominent men shared ownership of the steamboat *Hecla*, which ran aground at the mouth of the Gabouri Creek. In the fall of 1824, James Purdon sued the partners and former partners in this unfortunate venture for failure to make good on a promissory note. Purdon claimed that Henry Elliott, who had recently died, was master and commander of the *Hecla* on September 9, 1822, when he purchased supplies from Purdon and promised to pay him $130.33. Elliott's business partners included Ferdinand Rozier, Archibald Gamble, Peter Daguet, and Charles Gregoire, who took charge of selling the boat for salvage. Gregoire agreed to pay Purdon the amount he demanded in his lawsuit.[4]

Ferdinand Rozier later bought an interest in the steamboat *Vandalia*. Rozier and his descendants had a very strong connection to Ste. Genevieve's history. He came to the area in 1811 with John James Audubon, who later won fame for his paintings of American birds. Audubon disliked Ste. Genevieve and soon moved on, but Rozier stayed and became a very successful merchant. In 1837 his seventeen-year-old son, Firmin, took a job as a clerk on the *Vandalia*. Although he worked on the river for only a few months, his father decided to invest in the boat and used it to transport iron and lead from the mining areas west of Ste. Genevieve down the Mississippi to New Orleans. On return trips, the boat carried supplies for Rozier's mercantile business. Sometimes the elder Rozier rode as a passenger. The fate of the *Vandalia* is unknown. Firmin Rozier became a very prominent local citizen, opening a bank and later serving in the Missouri State Senate.[5]

Another notable French family opened a trading firm in association with their kinsman Pierre Menard, who lived at Kaskaskia, near the present-day town of Chester, Illinois, on the east bank of the river. In 1817, Jean-Baptiste Valle helped to establish the trading firm of Menard and Valle. His youngest son, Felix, joined the company in the 1820s. In

1824, the family purchased a stone building, which Felix, his wife, Odile, and their children occupied as a residence while using a portion of it as a store. After his father's death in 1849, Felix became the sole owner of the family's enterprises. By the time he died in 1877, he was the wealthiest man in Ste. Genevieve. His widow inherited hundreds of thousands of dollars and gave much of it to the local Catholic church. She also donated land for parks, a cemetery, and schools. Long after her passing in 1894, local citizens remembered her as "Mama Valle."[6]

After 1830, German immigrants formed a significant segment of the population in the settlements of the Mississippi valley, including Ste. Genevieve. Gottfried Duden, who toured America in the 1820s, published reports praising the soil in the bottoms of this great river and adding, "And what areas could be better situated for communication with the world than the banks of the Mississippi?" He particularly urged his countrymen to settle on the west bank of the river in the state of Missouri, and he also recommended traveling by riverboat. Following Duden's advice, German-speaking people found their way to Ste. Geneviev, built homes, attended church, and joined in the economic and social life of the old French town.[7]

German immigrants often joined in the commerce that the riverboats created. Typical of these new arrivals was Matthew Kern, who came from Baden in the late 1830s and became a naturalized American citizen in 1844. Matthew opened the Landing Hotel and operated a horse-drawn omnibus to bring visitors from the riverfront down the winding road into town. By the 1860s, he had built a new hotel and started a carriage line to convey passengers from Ste. Genevieve to the nearby town of Farmington three times a week.[8]

Steamboats brought trade goods to merchants and household goods to residents, but they also brought cholera to Ste. Genevieve. In October 1832, a riverboat dumped stricken passengers on the landing near the town. Dr. Lewis Linn, a local physician who would later become a U.S. senator, treated sufferers in his home. For the next year, the disease continued to plague residents of the town. Linn and another physician, Ichabod Sargent, did their best, given the state of medical knowledge at that time, to heal the sick. The remedies they used included bleeding (taking blood from the patient), sweating (placing the patients' feet in warm water or placing warm stones in their beds), and easing pain with laudanum. These treatments could not have cured the stricken people, who were probably dehydrated from vomiting and diarrhea, and in the first week of October 1833, there were nine deaths from the disease. Linn himself came down with cholera, but he recovered.[9]

During the 1849 epidemic that devastated St. Louis, the people of Ste. Genevieve also suffered from the contagion. Although Jean-Baptiste Valle died of old age, two other Valle family members and five of their slaves died of cholera during that terrible summer. In the twelve months preceding the 1850 census, seventy-eight local residents died, but the records regarding cause of death are sketchy. At least sixteen children and six adults died from unknown or unrecorded causes. In Memorial Cemetery, the grave marker of Martin Sweek and his wife, Caroline, bore this chilling inscription: "The above named persons / Died of cholera leaving / A family of 12 children."[10]

The river dragged many drowned men and women to the landing at Ste. Genevieve. In the 1840s and 1850s, a local man named Peter Moro supplemented his income by pulling corpses from the Mississippi and nearby creeks. On some occasions Moro participated in county coroner's inquests. In July 1846, the state of Missouri requested Moro and five other "good and honorable men" to collect and examine a body that had turned up in the river. Another record from April 1850 documents a similar transaction, in which the state paid for Moro's services. Other papers in the Sainte Genevieve Archives indicate that Moro and his son John regularly took part in the grim rituals of anonymous death.[11]

Between 1823 and 1868, more than twenty steamboats met with disaster at or near Ste. Genevieve. Numerous boats got tangled in underwater branches or tree stumps, called snags. These snagged vessels included the *Franklin* (1819), the *Cincinnati* (1823), the *Mississippi* (1825), the *New Jersey* (1830), the *Champlain* (1834), the *Oregon* (1841), the *Rubicon* (1841), the *Tennessee Valley* (1843), the *Corsair* (1844), the *Lander* (1844), the *Mendota* (1848), the *Cambria* (1851), the *Dunkirk* (1852), the *Huntsville* (1854), and the *Hindoo* (1855); there were no fatalities. But when the *Cutter* hit a snag on January 7, 1852, seven people died. Fires and collisions happened less frequently but often proved deadly. When the *Keokuk* burned on August 29, 1841, twelve people lost their lives, and when the *Sultan* went up in flames on April 2, 1858, twenty-three people perished. On March 21, 1844, the *Weston* collided with the *Aliquippa*, and three people died.[12]

The deadliest of all the steamboat disasters at Ste. Genevieve occurred when a boiler collapsed on the *Doctor Franklin No. 2* on August 22, 1852. *Lloyd's Steamboat Directory* for 1856 reported that the accident took place about five miles above Ste. Genevieve. Thirty-two passengers and crew members who happened to be on deck behind the engine died in the boiler's scalding water. The passengers in the cabin escaped with their lives. Firmin Rozier published an account of the catastrophe in his *History of the Early Settlement of the Mississippi Valley* in 1890. He stated that the flue collapsed at Turkey Island (near Chester, Illinois). The water that billowed over the deck pushed the vessel's two engineers into the river. Other people jumped overboard and drowned.[13]

As rescuers towed the boat to the Ste. Genevieve wharf, terrified survivors screamed in the cabin. Local citizens tended to the injured and, according to Rozier, buried the dead in a mass grave in Memorial Cemetery. Twenty-four of the dead were identified; others remained unknown. Chief engineer Robert McMurty was reported missing; third engineer George Hardy died. On the day after the disaster, the body of an unknown white man floated down from Turkey Island to the Little Rock Ferry Landing. Ste. Genevieve County Coroner M. J. Amoureux held an inquest on the same day. The coroner's jury determined that the man, who was about thirty-five years old, had been a passenger on the *Dr. Franklin No. 2* and died as a result of the explosion.[14]

Other poor souls who washed up on the banks at Ste. Genevieve included runaway slaves. Because Missouri was a slave state, those fugitives that didn't drown sometimes found themselves in the local jail. A notice in the *Missouri Republican* newspaper on January 4, 1850, announced that a sixteen-year-old boy calling himself "General," who stood five feet high and wore an old cloth hat, was in custody. His two owners, named Conner and McAfee, lived in Memphis and St. Louis. The notice stated that if these two men did not claim their property, he would be sold at the courthouse door in Ste. Genevieve.[15]

Free black people living in the community feared losing their liberty during the turbulent decade before the Civil War. For instance, the family of Louis Cavelier changed its surname to Louison. Name changes frequently occurred in the history of black families, who wanted to make it difficult for authorities to trace them and take away their freedom. Louis and his wife maintained their status as free people, remained in Ste. Genevieve, and weathered the crisis of the Civil War.[16]

During the war, Ste. Genevieve was a divided community. The old French families and the Anglo Americans were, in many cases, slave owners and Southern sympathizers, but most of the German American residents stood firm for the Union. During one wild night in February 1862, a group of noisy men and boys rode around town in a wagon, yelling "Hurrah for the Union," cursing and insulting passersby, and waving the American flag in people's faces. A local newspaper identified the carousers by German surnames and called them "Teutons." Men and boys from Ste. Genevieve served on both sides during the war.[17]

After the war, access to cheap river transportation supported the development of stone quarries and lime kilns in and around Ste. Genevieve. By the 1870s, several large sandstone quarries, employing hundreds of men, operated about four miles south of town. These quarries provided construction materials for the Eads Bridge. "Quicklime" (calcium carbonate) found in the bluffs north of Ste. Genevieve provided a valuable ingredient for making cement, an industry that took off in the late nineteenth and early twentieth centuries. In the 1920s, Mississippi Lime Company opened a limestone quarry and built several kilns. The company remained in business into the twenty-first century.[18]

The killing of two men who worked at the lime kiln in October 1930 revealed racial tensions in the community and also the wild side of life along the river. Henry Panchot and Paul Ritter went out in Ritter's car on a Saturday night, October 11, looking for excitement among the shacks near the Frisco Railroad depot tracks at the foot of Merchant Street. Two black men and a black woman apparently asked Panchot and Ritter for a ride to a craps game at Little Rock Ferry Landing. The black men, who were later identified as J. B. Lee and Guy Taylor, worked at the Mill Quarry. The woman, Vera Rogers, was just passing through town. When the car arrived at the landing, everyone got out. Lee and Taylor apparently took ten dollars, a watch, and a fountain pen from Ritter and Panchot, and then there was shooting.[19]

Panchot died immediately of gunshot wounds, but Ritter lived for two days after the incident. Witnesses watched from a boat as his assailants threw him into the river. His body floated a few hundred feet to a barge that Prohibition agents had recently seized from moonshiners. The federal agents pulled him from the water and contacted his brother, who took him to a hospital in St. Louis. In the meantime, Lee and Taylor fled in Ritter's car and hid out in the quarry. A local posse soon found Vera

Rogers hiding in a nearby house. After eight hours of questioning, she confessed to the crime. By eight o'clock in the morning, the sheriff's men had also found Taylor and Lee. In his hospital bed, Ritter told police that it was Lee who drew a pistol and did the shooting.[20]

In the aftermath of the homicide, white residents of Ste. Genevieve rose up in rage, and the National Guard arrived just in time to prevent a triple lynching. Taylor, Lee, and Rogers were moved to the city jail in St. Louis while angry white mobs harassed and threatened the town's old established black families and newcomers alike. After Ritter's death on Tuesday evening, the Guard had to come back to town to restore order. Local law enforcement officials arrested nine white men for terrorizing Louis Rebeau (or Ribault), a black mail carrier, who lived on St. Mary's Road. In the horrifying days after the killing, all but three black families left Ste. Genevieve. One week after the incident, the Guard turned over its peacekeeping responsibility to members of the American Legion. After passions died down, local whites invited black residents to return, and some of them did. But the black population of Ste. Genevieve dwindled almost to zero in the ensuing years.[21]

Racial tensions lingered after the incident on the riverbank. A sensitive young woman who visited Ste. Genevieve several times in the 1930s recalled years later that the old French town was very interesting, but she felt uncomfortable with the racial attitudes there. "When I would walk down a sidewalk in Ste. Genevieve," she told an interviewer, "black people—there weren't many—would get off into the street and let me pass.... That would upset me, something was not right." This young woman, who used the single name Martyl, later became a successful artist. In 1941, she painted a mural entitled "*La Guignolee*" in the Ste. Genevieve Post Office. The *Guignolee* (or *Guillonee*) was a New Year's celebration peculiar to the French colonies in North America.[22]

Ste. Genevieve's French heritage, along with its scenic location, drew many artists to the community. Martyl came along with her mother, Aimee Schweig, who was one of the founders of the Ste. Genevieve Artists' Colony and Summer School during the Great Depression. Local artist Mathew Ziegler provided housing and studio space for an impressive number of artists in the Shaw House, a historic building that his family owned. Thomas Hart Benton, Joe Jones, and others spent time at the colony and painted local subjects. Most of the artists, like Benton and Jones, were social realists or regionalists, who had an interest in painting the grittier side of life. Martyl painted a realistic scene of lime miners at work. Ziegler photographed workers on riverboats and painted a landscape entitled "Mississippi in Winter," showing the river covered with ice.[23]

In the mid-twentieth century, historians and architectural historians became fascinated with Ste. Genevieve as the best-preserved example of an old French settlement in the Mississippi River valley. Charles Peterson, founder of the Historic American Buildings Survey (HABS), recognized the unique character of the colonial vertical log houses and traced their roots to rural France. Only a very small number of such dwellings survive in modern times. In 1960, a National Park Service (NPS) team studying French exploration and settlement of North America concluded that of all the French colonial villages, trading posts, and forts along the Mississippi, only Ste. Genevieve has retained much of its early appearance.[24]

Despite the threat of flooding, admirers of the town's architectural heritage made concerted efforts to preserve the old French houses, opening some of them to the public. In 1956–1957, Dr. Ernest Allen Connally supervised the restoration of the Bolduc House, which has been owned and maintained for many years by the National Society of the Colonial Dames of America in the State of Missouri. Missouri's Department of Natural Resources restored and opened the Felix Valle State Historic Site in the 1970s. Historically important resources currently under state stewardship are the Jacob Phillipson House (also known as the Felix Valle House), the Bossier Warehouse (also known as the Shaw House), the Jean Baptiste St. Gemme Beauvais House (also called the Amoureux House), and the Delassus-Kern House (also known as the Kern House). Private individuals have also lovingly restored many of the old French houses, including the home of Jean-Baptiste Valle.

In the summer of 1993, Bernard and Vion Schram sat on the front porch of Valle's spacious log house and watched the overflow from the Mississippi River creep close to their front door. During that terrible year of flooding, volunteers raced to fill sandbags to hold back the surging water. Even so, the river wandered more than a mile from its banks, covering farmers' fields, forcing more than a hundred families to evacuate their homes, and flowing into some of the oldest of the vertical log houses on St. Mary's Road. After the water receded, federal and state governments cooperated in efforts to repair historic buildings and build a more effective levee system. Two years later, when the river flooded again, the levee saved the historic town.[25]

In the 1790s, the people of Ste. Genevieve had moved their town to higher ground, away from the dangerous river. Two centuries later, the river followed, reminding them just how dangerous it could be.

CHAPTER FOUR

Pilots

Inside the pilothouse
From the Collection of the Cape River Heritage Museum, Cape Girardeau

Your true pilot cares nothing about anything on earth but the river, and his pride in his occupation surpasses the pride of kings.

—Mark Twain, *Life on the Mississippi*

In the days of steamboating, pilots had a mystique surpassing that of any other person on the Mississippi. Captains were the masters of the boats, but pilots were the masters of the river. They learned the name of every town, the shape of every bend, the position of every sandbar, and the depth of every channel on their particular stretch of muddy water.

They could sense what was ahead of them, even in the dark, and they could steer the boat away from danger. People's lives depended upon the pilot's understanding of the feel and smell and power of the current. When the pilot was off duty, he could change into his best clothes, slick down his hair, and go into one of the river towns, where people gave him a hero's welcome.[1]

The pilot's swagger impressed lots of young men, including one with stooping shoulders and unruly hair who traveled from Cincinnati to New Orleans on the steamboat *Paul Jones* in 1857. Soon after boarding, he found his way to the pilothouse, took a seat on a big bench in the back, and began asking questions. At first the pilot, Horace Bixby, ignored his visitor, but gradually the young man, whose name was Samuel Clemens, got Bixby's attention by delivering a long, amusing monologue in a Missouri drawl. By the time the boat reached New Orleans, the two men had made a bargain. Clemens agreed to pay Bixby the exorbitant sum of five hundred dollars, and Bixby agreed to take him on as a cub pilot and teach him how to navigate the Mississippi.[2]

Several months later, Bixby headed west to ply his trade on the Missouri River, while Clemens continued his training under William Brown, who piloted the steamboat *Pennsylvania*. Clemens's younger brother Henry went to work as a "mud clerk" on that boat. The "mud clerk" held a very humble position, several levels down in the hierarchy from the purser (or chief clerk). One night, while the boat was docked in St. Louis, Clemens had a premonition. In his dream, he saw Henry lying in a casket, wearing Samuel's clothing, with a bouquet of roses on his chest. Within a day or two, the brothers made the trip from St. Louis to New Orleans. Clemens had a falling-out with the pilot, who ordered him to leave the boat. Henry continued on the trip to Ship Island, below Memphis, where the *Pennsylvania*'s boilers exploded. His older brother followed on another boat, arriving in Memphis to find Henry lying on the floor in a makeshift infirmary with about forty other burned and wounded victims of the disaster.[3]

For about a week, Clemens stayed with his younger brother as he lay dying. One physician held out hope that he would survive, but his body was badly scalded. On the night before his death, the attending physicians accidentally gave him an overdose of morphine. As Clemens recalled many years later, Henry died early in the morning. Clemens went away for a while to get some sleep, and when he came back to the morgue,

Henry lay in a casket, dressed in a suit of his brother's clothing. An elderly lady entered the room and placed a bouquet of roses on his chest.[4]

During the winter of 1858–1859, Clemens served as a pilot on the *A. B. Chambers No. 2,* running between St. Louis and New Orleans. Grant Marsh, the first mate, said that Clemens was not a great pilot, but he had courage. Marsh recalled one incident, in particular, when Clemens saved the lives of several roustabouts. On a very cold day, the boat ran aground near the town of Commerce, Missouri, about 165 miles south of St. Louis. Efforts to move the boat back into the channel failed, and the fuel ran out. The captain ordered Marsh and Clemens and several oarsmen to take a small boat to Commerce and haul back some wood to burn in the boat's furnaces. On the trip upriver, the small boat had to dodge ice floes. Marsh shouted to Clemens to turn back, but Clemens ordered the crew to row with all their strength to the Missouri bank. A huge icy swell rose behind them as the boat sped safely to the shore. If Clemens had turned back, the boat and the men would have been crushed.[5]

Clemens's skills improved so much that Bixby accepted him as a partner, and he worked steadily for the next few years. Between 1858 and 1861, he served on several boats, including the *New Falls City,* the *Aleck Scott,* and the *Alonzo Child.* At this time in his life, he was a clean-shaven and smooth-faced young man, who smoked and constantly told jokes but never smiled. Although he was relatively quiet and retiring, he was popular with officers and crew members. He had proven his courage, but he abandoned the river during the turmoil of the Civil War. Bixby said that, during the early months of the war, Clemens had to run blockades. On one occasion, near Jefferson Barracks, just south of St. Louis, bullets pierced the smokestacks of Twain's boat. "After that," said Bixby, "my pilot went west."[6]

Many years later, Captain Louis Rosche commented wryly on Clemens, by then writing as Mark Twain, and his decision to give up the life of a river pilot and turn, first to an adventure in the West, and then to the life of a professional writer. Rosche had worked on the *Oceanic* under Horace Bixby and admired him tremendously. "The cub trained by him," said Rosche, "was fortunate indeed." Rosche recalled that many of his colleagues found it difficult to understand why Twain would "leave the wheel of a steamboat to push a pen, especially after learning the piloting business under one of the best teachers on the river." But Rosche had to admit, tongue in cheek, that Twain's literary work was "right readable."[7]

Sobieski ("Beck") Jolly was one man who never wanted to give up the life of a river pilot. His father, John Jolly, began his career on flatboats and eventually became a master of Ohio and Mississippi steamboats. All three of his sons grew up to be pilots. Sobieski, born in 1831, first served as a cub pilot on the steamer *Palestine* in 1846. During his three years of training, his instructors were his father, his older brother Alsabid, and two uncles, Joseph C. and Alex C. Smith. Jolly piloted steamboats on the Ohio and Mississippi rivers between Cincinnati and New Orleans for a few years and then found work on the steamer *Pacific* plying the Mississippi River between St. Louis and New Orleans.[8]

During the Civil War, Jolly served on several boats that transported troops, ammunition, and supplies for the Union. On one occasion, when he was working on the *C. E. Hillman*, his young wife, Emma, was onboard. He recalled in an unpublished memoir that a band of guerrillas came out of the woods and fired on the boat. Bullets broke glass and went through the boat's chimneys. His wife was standing behind an iron barricade placed around the pilothouse, when a bullet cut the cord of a bell above her head. One of the boat's officers pulled her down inside the protective circle of metal and advised her to stay put.[9]

After the war, Jolly worked on several of the great floating palaces, including the *Thompson Dean*, the *Great Republic*, and the *James Howard*. For two seasons in the early 1880s, he served as master of the U.S. snagboat *R. E. DeRussy*, but he preferred working on the packet boats. As the glory days of the steamboats waned, he went to work on the towboats *Jay Gould* and *John Gilmore*. Near the end of his career, he served as master, pilot, and clerk aboard railroad transfer ferries. By 1900, he had retired from his life on the river.[10]

Between 1898 and 1901, living in retirement with his family in St. Louis, Jolly wrote a memoir for his son, Percy, who lived at home and worked as a bookkeeper. Realizing that he was nearing the end of his life, Jolly wanted his son to know that he felt a great pride in his long years of working on the river. It was difficult for most people to understand, he wrote, "what a responsible position a pilot stands in while on duty at the wheel. What a memory to locate every obstruction, detect any change of channel, [and] locate all landings [on] the darkest of nights." Jolly died in St. Louis on June 5, 1905, leaving behind a wife, a son, and a handwritten record of devotion to his craft. "The older I become," he wrote, "the prouder I am to know that the profession of a pilot is a grand one."[11]

Because of his association with Twain, Horace Bixby became the best-known pilot on the Mississippi River, and he almost certainly was one of the best. Like Jolly, he never wanted any other life. Born in Geneseo, New York, in 1826, he ran away to Cincinnati at the age of eighteen and worked as a mud clerk on the steamer *Olivia.* By the time he turned twenty, he had become a pilot, and within a few years he was earning up to five hundred dollars a month. This was the great era of steamboating, and pilots were among the aristocrats of the river trade. Bixby renewed his pilot's license on the day before he died in 1912 at the age of eighty-six. He lives on, in somewhat fictionalized form, in Twain's famous *Life on the Mississippi.*[12]

Twain recalled one of his first trips as Bixby's cub pilot going downriver from St. Louis to Cairo, a two-hundred-mile trip, when the water was low. He learned on this trip that traveling upriver was relatively easy, but going downriver was perilous, especially at night. A good pilot, he realized, had to learn not only the locations of every town and bend but also "every old snag and one-limbed cotton wood and obscure wood-pile" along hundreds of miles of river. Bixby knew the river and was not afraid of it. On one memorable night, Twain and other would-be pilots watched in awe as Bixby guided the boat over the dangerous shoals at Hat Island near Grand Tower, Illinois. In *Life on the Mississippi*, Twain vividly evoked the tension he felt as the watchmen called out the changing depths of the water, "Half-twain! Quarter twain, Mark twain..." and then "Seven feet! Six-and..." The boat touched bottom, and quickly, unflinchingly, Bixby rang the bells, demanded more speed, and maneuvered the boat past the danger. A shout of joy went up, and one of Bixby's admirers said, "By the Shadow of Death, but he's a lightning pilot!"[13]

As a young man Bixby was a bit of a dandy, wearing a tall hat and yellow gloves, and he developed a reputation as a daredevil. "They said I was foolhardy," he recalled later in his life. "But I was always sure of myself. Certainly I should have lost many a boat if it had not been so. I have many times brought my vessel through difficult places on bad nights when other Captains were tied to the bank; but the risk never seemed great. I always felt that it was the duty of a pilot to pilot." People who met him as an older man described him as small, energetic, and wiry, with a piercing look in his arresting blue eyes.[14]

Bixby enhanced his reputation with his Civil War service as a gunboat pilot during the Union campaigns to capture Island Number 10, Memphis, and Vicksburg and gain control of commerce on the Mississippi River. In the early months of 1862, after Grant won victories at Fort Henry and Fort Donnellson, the Confederates fell back to a line extending across the river from Corinth, Mississippi, to Island Number 10, on a bend just above the town of New Madrid, Missouri. Union soldiers commanded by General John A. Pope and naval forces under Commodore Andrew H. Foote quickly pursued the enemy downriver. In March 1862, Foote left Cairo with nine gunboats, including the *St. Louis,* Eads's famous *Carondelet,* and a less powerful boat, the *Benton,* piloted by Bixby.[15]

On March 15, 1862, the day after New Madrid fell to the Union, Foote's gunboats appeared around the bend of the river and began firing on Confederate batteries. During this bombardment, the *Benton* was hit four times, and an explosion on the *St. Louis* killed two men and wounded several others. There was, it turned out, a serious design flaw in the ironclads. When they were anchored at the stern, their paddlewheels caused them to move about wildly, making accurate shooting impossible. The men onboard were in constant danger of explosions like the one onboard the *St. Louis,* and the boats could not back up and move upstream against the river's current.[16]

Between April 4 and April 7, the *Carondelet* and the *Pittsburgh* made daring nighttime runs past the enemy stronghold on Island Number 10. At a crucial moment, the *Carondelet*'s smokestacks burst into flames, revealing her presence to the Confederate batteries. Running at full speed, the gunboat made it past the island. Two nights later, the *Pittsburgh* accomplished the same daring feat, and soon after that, the two gunboats attacked the Rebel batteries. By noon on April 7, the Confederates on Island No. 10 surrendered to Pope's infantry, which crossed the Mississippi with the protection of the gunboats, including the *Benton,* that were still waiting upstream. Among the boats captured in this fight was the CSS *Red Rover*, which was sent to Cairo, repaired, and used for a Union hospital ship.[17]

Two months later, the *Benton* played a role in the Union's victory at Memphis. At daybreak on June 6, the *Benton*, the *Carondelet,* the *St. Louis,* and the *Cairo* led the attack on a line of eight Confederate ironclads ranged above the city. During a chaotic scramble, with guns blazing on all sides, the Union gunboats destroyed one Confederate boat and captured two others. This victory gave the North control of the river north of Vicksburg, Mississippi, but the struggle for control of Vicksburg would be long and hard. Bixby's ten months of service on the Union's gunboat fleet would end before that battle was won.[18]

After the war, Bixby rose from the position of pilot to that of captain, and he returned for a short time to the Missouri River, where his colleague Grant Marsh was rapidly making a name for himself. On April 1, 1865, Bixby was piloting the steamboat *Bertrand* when it hit a snag and sank about fifty miles above Omaha, Nebraska. Passengers and crew all made it safely to the bank, but the boat and cargo were totally lost. This incident may have contributed to his dislike of the shallow waters and sandbars of the Missouri. In 1866, he took the steamer *Rubicon* to Montana and found that he had to turn around and go back to St. Louis, because the deep-water boat could not make it farther upstream. After that he confined his efforts to the Mississippi. Rivermen later dubbed him "the Grant Marsh of the Lower Mississippi." Bixby accepted it as a compliment, saying, of Marsh, "Any man who can run a boat for twenty years in that rainwater creek [the Missouri River] above Bismarck is surely the king of pilots."[19]

As a captain, Bixby had a reputation for keeping strict discipline. Louis Rosche shipped with him as an up-and-coming young mate on the steamer *Oceanic*. Rosche had a hot temper, and the two of them did not get along. One day, while they were getting the boat ready for departure, Bixby pointed to a crowbar and ordered Rosche to fetch it. Bristling at the captain's brusque tone, Rosche leaned down slowly and picked up the bar. Bixby took offense at his attitude and said, "Don't be all day about it. Hand it here."

Rosche shouted back at him, "I'm no common roustabout, sir, and I'll not be talked to that way. Here, take your damned iron." He threw the crowbar down at the captain's feet and immediately went to his cabin to pack his things. He knew he was finished on the *Oceanic*. In spite of this bad experience, Rosche believed that Bixby was one of the best pilots on the river and a competent captain.[20]

He was also a family man. In 1860 he married Susan Weibling of New Orleans. She traveled with him at least some of the time. Apparently, she was onboard the steamboat *Bertrand* when it hit the fatal snag. Bixby, his wife, and a servant registered at the Herndon House in Omaha on Sunday, April 2, 1865, the day after the wreck. Within two years, both she and her child had died. On January 2, 1868, Bixby married Mary Sheble, daughter of Captain Edwin A. Sheble, a prominent riverman, of St. Louis. The couple had three children, Edwina (born ca. 1872), Edwin (born ca. 1874), and George Mason (born in 1877). Edwina frequently accompanied her father on trips, including the time when he revisited the river with Mark Twain in 1882. At that time, she was not yet ten years old.[21]

After the Civil War and the sinking of the *Bertrand*, Bixby experienced more success and more disasters. In the 1870s, he became a principal stockholder in the Anchor Line, which operated a fleet of large and elaborate boats between St. Louis and New Orleans. He captained numerous boats, including the *City of Alton*, which burned at St. Louis in January of 1884. When his floating palace the *City of Baton Rouge* sank at Hermitage, Louisiana, on December 12, 1890, two passengers drowned. These losses, plus the general decline of steamboat traffic, caused the Anchor Line to fade away. But Bixby did not want to give up his life on the river. He went into government service as the captain of the snagboat *Horatio G. Wright* and remained in that position until a year before he died.[22]

In early June 1902, Twain and Bixby met at the Planters' Hotel in St. Louis and talked about old times. After a long chat, the two men walked across Fourth Street to the Pilots' Association headquarters, where Bixby and the famous author joined other old rivermen, including Beck Jolly and John Henton Carter ("Commodore Rollingpin"). Like Twain, Carter had left the river for the writing life. Reporters asked Bixby if Twain had ever paid the five hundred dollars for his pilot's training. Bixby said he paid three hundred of it, and then the war started, and he did not have the rest of the money. At the time of this friendly reunion, the debt had long since been forgiven.[23]

Bixby often said he wanted to "die in harness," and he nearly got his wish. At the age of eighty-six, he renewed his pilot's license and was planning to pilot the towboat *Nokomis*. As he always did, he got up early in the morning, got dressed, and was waiting for the call to take out the boat. If the call came, he did not respond. His wife came home and found him dead in bed on Thursday, August 1, 1912. The coroner said he died of apoplexy. Funeral services were held at the home of his daughter, Edwina, and her husband, Louis Pim. The old captain was laid to rest in St. Louis's Bellefontaine Cemetery after sixty-six years of continuous service on the river.[24]

Another pilot who served for many decades on the river was George Clark, who died in St. Louis in 1923 at the age of eighty-three. During the Civil War, Clark served in the Union navy. After the war, he went to Cairo, which was a hub for of the lumber industry. Reportedly, he "wore out" three towboats pulling barges piled with logs. People in Cairo remembered him as a snappy dresser who won the admiration of local boys who wanted to follow in his footsteps. When he was in town he frequently took fifteen or twenty children with him to the picture show. Like other pilots of the steamboat era, Clark had a romantic aura that appealed to the spirits of the young.[25]

Elbert L. "Wamp" Poe of Cape Girardeau began a sixty-three-year career in 1910, a transitional year, when old-time steamboats traveled the river along with towboats and barges. During his many decades on the river, he worked as both a pilot and an engineer. He remembered a time when pilots communicated to the engine room with speaking tubes and bells. "You had a pretty good-size bell, string running to the pilot house," he said in an interview in 1980. "And it was a stop-and-come-ahead bell. Then you had a smaller chime bell. It was a backup and a dead-slow bell. Then you had a gong." By the end of his career, of course, methods of

The fascinating river
From the Collection of the Cape River Heritage Museum, Cape Girardeau

navigation and communication had dramatically changed. Before Poe's death in 1984, a few of his reflections on the life of a pilot were captured in Jane Curry's book about pilots, *The River's in My Blood.* [26]

Poe's son, E. A., "Li'l Wamp," who followed in his footsteps, remembered the pride his father felt in his profession. The old-time pilots like his father were different from the ones in E. A.'s generation, or so he believed. These older men, he said, cared about the river. "What's good for the river is good for them. Some of these younger people, it's just a job, you know. They could care less." He regretted the change. "There's something different, too. You know Dad, when he got his license he was literally proud of it. Still proud of it...." But some of that pride was missing, he thought, in younger men. "They're interested in the money. But they don't really care about the river as such."[27]

Still, E. A. admitted, there was something about working on the river, something that went beyond the money. "If a man works on the river," he said in an interview, "you do an awful lot of traveling, and it's amazing how different this country really is." He tried to explain this feeling. "It's amazing to me how much you really learn about the country and the people ... how different they are."[28]

Maybe this was why his father kept working until 1973, when he was seventy-seven years old. It was hard to leave the river. Mark Twain said a true pilot cared about nothing on earth but the river, and that seems to be partially false, but it also seems to be partially true.

CHAPTER FIVE

Chester, Illinois

The Popeye statue near Chester Bridge
Photograph by Bonnie Stepenoff

We found a railway intruding at Chester, Illinois; Chester has also a penitentiary now, and is otherwise marching on.

—Mark Twain, *Life on the Mississippi*

The town of Chester and the old French village of Kaskaskia shared the rich bottomland at the confluence of the Kaskaskia River and the Mississippi. French settlers first occupied the heavily wooded lowland in 1703. Many of these early French inhabitants were boatmen, who transported goods on the river between Canada and New Orleans. These were hardy men who traveled the river in long, narrow *pirogues* or flat-bottomed *bateaux*. By mid-century, the wealthier residents were bringing elaborate clothing with diamond buttons and silver buckles from the port of New Orleans. After the Seven Years War ended in 1763, the old French settlement became part of the British Empire, and in 1795, Kaskaskia became the first seat of government in Illinois Territory and also the seat of Randolph County.[1]

One prominent local citizen was Canadian-born Pierre Menard, who formed a business connection with the Valle family of Ste. Genevieve. He opened a store on the east bank of the river in 1791. Before he became a naturalized citizen of the United States, he served in Illinois' territorial legislature. When Illinois became a state, Menard was chosen as lieutenant governor. His vertical log home survived into the twenty-first century as a remnant of the region's French heritage.[2]

As more and more English-speaking people arrived in the area, the land on the east bank of the Mississippi became known as the American Bottoms. Among the new arrivals was Samuel Smith, who operated a ferry and built the first house in Chester in 1829. He named the new settlement after his wife's hometown in England. The town of Chester was incorporated in 1835 and became a landing for ferryboats coming from the west bank. After the 1844 flood ravaged Kaskaskia, turning it into an island, Chester became the Randolph County seat.[3]

In the mid-nineteenth century, Chester developed as a shipping and stopping point on the river. An unusual commodity shipped upriver to St. Louis and downriver to New Orleans from Chester was castor oil. A local citizen named Richard B. Servant became one of the wealthiest men in Randolph County by convincing local farmers to grow castor beans. The farmers sold the beans to Servant, who extracted the oil using presses powered by horses. Castor oil had many uses in soaps, lubricants, dyes, and as a famously bad-tasting medicine (chiefly a laxative) for children. The local firm of Holmes, Swanwick, and Company also dealt extensively in castor beans. Gradually, the discovery of petroleum and the development of petroleum oils made the castor-bean industry obsolete.[4]

During the second half of the nineteenth century, the Mississippi River continued to encroach on the bottomlands near Chester, moving closer to the channel of the Kaskaskia River. Decades of river traffic had deforested the riverbanks, as trees became fuel for steamboats. The state of Illinois attempted to control the Mississippi by constructing piers and other barriers, but heavy ice floes in the winter of 1880–1881 destroyed the protective structures. In April 1881, the Mississippi burst into the channel of the Kaskaskia, taking over the lower ten miles of the smaller river, and rearranging the local geography, moving Kaskaskia to the west bank of the Mississippi. As time went on, the river kept expanding its channel, gradually washing away most of the old French village. On the east bank, the town of Chester moved many of its buildings up to the bluffs and built a set of steps providing access to the river.[5]

The Mississippi river played an important role in the state's decision to build a prison in Chester in 1877. After considering sites in several other towns, officials chose a piece of land once owned by Pierre Menard between the river and the limestone bluffs about one mile from the center of Chester. Proximity to the river as well as to a railroad line was important because the prison, which was initially named the Southern Illinois Penitentiary and later called the Menard Correctional Center, was in part an industrial complex, designed to make use of inmate labor to make and ship products. While portions of the prison were still under construction, prisoners were put to work digging stone from the nearby quarries. In the 1880s the prison housed hundreds of men and a few women and assigned most of them to labor on the prison farm or in a shoe factory, plumbing and carpenter shops, a tin shop, a mattress factory, a paint shop, or a tobacco factory.[6]

Because of the prison, the people of Chester lived with an ever-present sense of danger. On a couple of hot days in July 1923, local citizens locked their doors, closed their shops, and stood guard with shotguns, after forty-two inmates escaped from Menard. By that time, the state had constructed an Asylum for Insane Criminals, which later became Chester State Hospital, on the prison grounds. During a brief period of outdoor exercise in a courtyard, a group of men from the asylum overpowered their guards and used a bench as a battering ram to break through the fence. One man attacked a guard with a butcher knife. Officials banned women and children from the streets of Chester, as sixty guards and a posse of citizens combed the area, eventually recapturing the fugitives. During the manhunt, the posse shot and killed William Jackson, a black man who had been imprisoned for murder.[7]

In the 1920s and 1930s, thousands of men worked in the enterprises associated with the prison. Donald Clemmer's book *The Prison Community,* published in 1940, documented life at Menard. During the 1930s, the inmate population averaged more than two thousand men between the ages of seventeen and ninety. Twenty percent of the inmates were black; none were Asian. Most were native-born; most of the rest were of Italian, German, Austrian, or Canadian origin. Nearly every able-bodied man worked at least part-time in the quarry, knitting mills, workshops, farm, laundry, bakery, or kitchen.[8]

More than six hundred men worked in the quarry in six gangs of one hundred men each. Two or three guards watched over each of the gangs—known by number as "1-Gang," "2-Gang," and so on. The work they did was hard and dirty. Some men removed surface soil with shovels. Others broke up large pieces of rock with sledgehammers and chisels. Still others pushed wheelbarrows full of rock to the cast-iron rail cars that carried the rock to and from the big crushing machinery. Between one-quarter and one-third of the quarry workers were black. In general, the more dangerous and unruly men were assigned to this backbreaking work.[9]

Riots and protests happened rarely, but the potential for violent upheaval always loomed. Clemmer witnessed an incident that originated with one of the work gangs. This particular gang of ninety men did such work as unloading food, coal, and lumber from the freight cars that came into the prison yard. On the day of the trouble, the guards ordered the men to keep on working after the whistle blew for the lunch break. Within a few minutes, the men started yelling, "Don't work! Don't work!" Most of the men stood idle. Some of them kept working but at a slow pace. A captain of the guards gathered the men and explained that they had to go back to work but that they would be fed later. Most of the men went back to work to a chorus of shouts and boos from the holdouts. The guards marched thirty-four of the men to solitary confinement. According to Clemmer, the causes of the protest were the semi-tyranny of the guards, the muggy weather, hunger, fatigue, and a general feeling of unrest. The strike failed, and most of the men returned to work, because their leadership was weak, and there was no strong feeling of unity within the gang. But anger seethed beneath the surface.[10]

The prison's gloomy presence surely influenced Chester's most famous local citizen, Elzie Crisler Segar, creator of Popeye, the Sailor Man. In many episodes of the Popeye cartoons, there is a gruff and menacing character named Bluto (aka Brutus). As a villain, he is not particularly conniving or intelligent, just doggedly intent on beating up Popeye and stealing his true love, Olive Oyl. Bluto always has the upper hand against the smaller and gentler man until Popeye eats a can of spinach and becomes physically powerful enough to win any fight. It is not difficult to connect Bluto to the imagination of a boy growing up in a town next to a prison filled with dangerous characters separated from the townfolk by fences and walls.

The river also had an influence on Segar and his comic creation. Born in 1894, Segar was the son of Amzi and Enna Segar, a German American couple who lived near the river bluff in Chester. As a child he fished and went rafting on the river. He and his friends found an island on which they could play. When he was ten years old, he used an old rowboat to ferry townspeople from the riverbank to the spot where a U.S. Navy ship was temporarily anchored. The sailors on the ship surely made an impression on the young boy's mind.[11]

As a teenager, Segar found many ingenious ways of making money. He worked at various times as a house painter, paper hanger, billboard artist, and window dresser. At the age of twelve, he began earning fifty cents a day working for J. William Schuchert, manager of the local movie theater known as the Chester Opera House. Segar played the drums while Jessie Lee Huffstutler played piano during silent movies. On Saturday mornings he used colored chalk to draw cartoons on the sidewalk advertising the latest film. He was also in charge of changing posters around town, drawing show bills to hand out in the theater, and creating advertising slides to be shown between reels of film. Eventually he learned to be a motion-picture projectionist.[12]

Schuchert paid for the mail-order art lessons that Segar took from the Evans Correspondence Course in Cartooning. When his instructor asked for one drawing, Segar would send eight or ten, and the instructor would patiently critique them. Segar finished the course in eighteen months and then went to Chicago, where he found work as a cartoonist for the *Chicago Herald.* Segar paid humorous tribute to Schuchert in the character of Popeye's friend Wimpy, who was always cadging hamburgers. Schuchert loved hamburgers and often sent his theater employees out to buy them from the Weibusch Saloon or the Ed Middendorf Confectionary in Chester.[13]

Popeye and Olive Oyl also had their counterparts in Chester. Many people believe that the model for Olive was a woman named Dora Paskel, who was very tall and thin and wore a bun at the nape of her neck. When Segar was a teenager, Dora was a woman in her twenties who was married to a merchant named Frank Paskel. The model for Popeye apparently was Frank "Rocky" Fiegel, a one-eyed, pipe-smoking rascal with a wiry frame, a jutting chin, and a pugnacious attitude. According to the 1920 census, he was an unmarried fifty-two-year-old man living with his eighty-year-old mother and working as a laborer on the streets of Chester. People remember him as a little guy who often got into fights at the Weibusch Saloon.[14]

When Segar introduced Popeye in a comic strip on January 17, 1929, the references to Chester were striking. One of the main characters in this strip was a fellow named Castor Oyl, harking back to Chester's days as a producer and shipper of this medicinal product. In the comic strip Castor Oyl has bought a big sailing boat and wants to take it out to Dice Island, where he hopes to make a fortune gambling. Segar spent time on an island playing with his boyhood friends, and they might have done some gambling there. Castor Oyl is searching for an experienced man to take charge of his boat. He scours the docks and finally comes upon a one-eyed man in a sailor suit with an anchor tattooed on his arm. "Hey there! Are you a sailor?" asks Castor Oyl. Popeye, the smart aleck, replies, "Ja think I'm a cowboy?"[15]

Popeye was a "sailor man," who worked at swabbing decks on a variety of vessels on unidentified bodies of water. The locations of his adventures ranged from wharves to carnivals, city streets to railroads in the Wild West. Popeye was never specifically associated with the ocean or with the seafaring life, and he could just as easily have been a man who worked on the river or walked the streets of Chester during Segar's childhood and youth.

Popeye's story is basically one of resiliency. The plots vary in detail, and the scenery constantly changes, but Olive remains true to her man, and Bluto tries to steal her away. Popeye and Bluto challenge each other to various contests of skill and strength. The contest is uneven until Popeye eats a can of spinach. Then, of course, he gains his strength and wins the fight. The same basic theme has been repeated thousands of times in comic strips, cartoons, and full-length movies based on Segar's characters. Sadly, Segar died in Los Angeles on October 14, 1938, at the age of forty-four, and other artists took over the Popeye franchise. But the story line remained the same. The underdog is nearly defeated, but finds the strength to win against the bully.[16]

The same story line could be applied to Chester's attempts to build a bridge across the Mississippi River. Townspeople started making plans when the automobile age was just beginning. In 1907, state highway officials used inmate labor to build and test a model bridge using gravel from the quarry at Menard. The highway bridge from Chester on the east bank to Perryville, Missouri, on the west bank of the river finally opened to traffic in 1942. Two years later a storm caused two sections of the bridge to collapse. Reconstruction of the sections took another two years, and the bridge reopened on August 24, 1946.[17]

Chester continued to face threats of violence from inmates at the prison. In late October 1952, inmates who worked in Menard's limestone quarry led a mutiny that resulted in a five-day siege. On the evening of October 27, after the prisoners had finished their work for the day and were marching back from the dining hall to the East Cell House, a group called the "6-Gang" captured seven guards and barricaded the doors of the cell block. Prison officials turned off all the electricity and allowed no food inside the captured building. More than three hundred inmates took part in the rebellion. In the early morning hours of October 31, Illinois governor Adlai E. Stevenson arrived at the prison and issued an ultimatum to the mutineers.[18]

When they refused to leave the building, about three hundred state troopers and prison guards stormed into the cell house with shotguns, machine guns, and clubs. Five of the hostages fought their way out and staggered into the prison yard hungry and dazed. The inmates released two other guards who had been locked in cells. During a thirty-seven-minute confrontation, only one prisoner was wounded. Governor Stevenson watched as guards led the rebellious prisoners back to their cells. In 1973 and again in 1974, smaller numbers of prisoners engaged in riots during a time when the overall population of the prison was growing. These problems drew growing attention to the prison and brought about reforms in the 1980s and 1990s.[19]

Another threat to Chester came directly from the river. During the great flood of 1993, the levee gave way just upriver from the prison, and water seeped into the northern sections of town. The mighty surge of water forced the bridge to close, so that the ten-minute crossing from Perryville to Chester turned into a six-hour journey until the bridge could be reopened. But damage in Chester was minor. Kaskaskia, or what remained of it, suffered much more. The old French village that barely survived the flood of 1844 and became separated from the mainland after the flood of 1881 finally faced extinction. About 125 people lived on

Kaskaskia Island up until the time of the 1993 flood, when water covered the entire village Kaskaskia survived, although the population dwindled to little more than a dozen.[20]

Chester's most famous native fictional son, Popeye, the Sailor Man, has become a national symbol of optimism and tenacity. He is not the biggest, handsomest, or smartest guy in the world, but he never gives up on his true love, and he never backs down from a fight. For the people who live in river towns, the character and his never-ending struggles have a clear connection to real life.

CHAPTER SIX

Mates, Deckhands, and Roustabouts

Unloading cargo
From the Collection of the Cape River Heritage Museum, Cape Girardeau

> "Hey there! Are you a sailor?
> "Ja think I'm a cowboy?"
>
> —Elzie Segar

In 1864, at the age of twelve, Louis Rosche secretly boarded a riverboat in hopes of landing a job as a deckhand. As he recalled many years later, he hid behind stacks of wheat in a dim, cluttered hold, staying as far as possible from the shaft of sunlight that entered through a square opening in the deck. He planned to wait until the boat backed away from the St. Louis levee and chugged out into the channel. Then he would declare his presence and ask the mate for a job. He had planned this during the many hours when he stood on the wharf watching the steamboats land and depart. Like many boys his age, he dreamed of being a pilot turning the big wheel or a captain wearing a white silk cap or a mate barking orders at the crew. But his plan went awry when two black roustabouts came down the ladder into the hold.[1]

One of the rousters dropped a sack of wheat onto the floor and raised a cloud of dust. Rosche could not suppress a sneeze, and the muscular man shouted at him, found his hiding place, and lifted him up into the air. The large black man carried the frightened boy up to the deck, grabbed him by the seat of his trousers, and indicated that he was going to toss him over the rail into the water. The boat was not far from the bank, but Rosche could not swim. The rouster's companion called him Big Jake and told him to let the white boy go. The two black men, suddenly ignoring the errant boy, started arguing and then squared off, ready to fight.[2]

At this point, the mate stepped in, grabbed an axe, and waded through the crowd of men that had gathered on deck. Tall and wiry with a crooked nose, the mate brandished the axe and demanded an end to the disturbance. But the captain, whom Rosche remembered as a "swell" in a tall hat and a brightly colored vest, opened his wallet and took out a hundred dollar bill, turned to a companion, and bet that the smaller black man would beat Big Jake in a fair fight. The mate deferred to the captain and acted as referee while the two men charged at each other and butted heads. After a short explosive contest, Big Jake lay flat on the deck, and one of the other roustabouts had to revive him with a bucket of cold water. The smaller man had smashed the hard part of his own head against the big man's temple, knocking him out. The captain gave the winner a five dollar bill.[3]

Then, turning to Rosche, the captain asked, "What have you to say for yourself?" Trembling with fear, the boy explained that he had stowed away because he wanted a job on the boat. The captain winked at his companion and asked how old Rosche was. He lied and said he was going on fifteen. With another wink, the captain said, "I don't think you are that old, but you are a fine, sturdily built lad, and you will be a big man some day. I notice you seem to be neat, too, although Big Jake has mussed you up a bit." He turned to the mate and told him to find a place for Rosche as a cabin boy or deck-sweep. When the captain walked away, the mate scowled and told the boy to go home, pack a bag, and come back at midnight when the boat would be casting off.[4]

It is certainly possible that Rosche exaggerated the drama of his initiation, but his story is consistent with factual accounts of life on the riverboats. This was a male world, in which crew members were known not by their names, but by nicknames like "Big Jake." Deck crew members, as a whole, were sometimes called "wharf rats." This was a world of transients, in which employment was seasonal, temporary, and dangerous. Workers would often come and go before anyone really got to know their real names or anything about them. Many of them entered this life as boys with dreams of becoming pilots or captains, and some of them, like Rosche, succeeded. But most of them drifted into other occupations or perished.[5]

As Rosche suggested, there was a strict hierarchy on a riverboat. The captain (sometimes called "The Old Man") was a "swell," who often owned or partially owned the boat. Pilots, clerks, engineers, and mates belonged to an elite class of officers, or skilled workers, roughly equivalent to the "management" in an industrial corporation. Among these managers, however, the mate occupied a position of lesser status. He had to show deference to the higher-ranking officers, but he could be high-handed or even abusive to the crew. In Rosche's story, the mate could not question the captain's orders, but he could turn and snarl at the crew member he had been forced to hire.[6]

There were two major divisions among the crew members. Cabin workers served as cooks, maids, waiters, stewards, porters, watchmen, and barbers. On boats carrying freight, the cabin crew attended to the officers' needs. On passenger boats, they were very much like the staff of a hotel. The cabin crew generally slept on carpeted floors outside the sleeping quarters. Deck workers included the firemen, who fueled the furnaces, in addition to deckhands, and roustabouts. Deckhands cleaned and swept the deck, measured the depth of the water for the pilot, and acted as watchmen. Roustabouts carried the freight on and off the boat, while deckhands often stowed the freight once it was onboard. Deck workers, in general, had to bed down on the main deck or in the hold amid the machinery and cargo.[7]

Before the Civil War, slaves and free black people often served on the same boats as white workers, although their work and sleeping spaces tended to be segregated. After the war, black and white people continued to work on the boats, but separation of the races also continued. Some boats had all-white or all-black cabin crews; some boats had mixed crews but assigned them to separate areas. Deckhands were generally white; roustabouts were often black. African Americans frequently worked as firemen. Assigning different tasks to different races tended to create segregated work spaces, but on small boats separation was not feasible. On larger boats, however, racial segregation was standard practice.[8]

Rosche's story encapsulates many facts of life for steamboat workers. According to many historians, harsh discipline and the threat of violence were daily occurrences. The mate brandishing an axe represented reality, not fiction. Historians have also confirmed that fighting, drinking, and gambling were part of steamboat culture. The head-butting fight between the two roustabouts and the captain's bet were also believable, if not strictly factual, events. Rosche must have been a tough and leathery character to survive and succeed in this dangerous world, which he entered at such a tender age.[9]

The rough and reckless culture of the crew men originated on the flatboats before the age of steam. Historian Michael Allen wrote that in river towns like St. Louis in the late eighteenth and early nineteenth centuries, runaway boys and idle young men loitered on the wharves looking for jobs as hands on any boat that would have them. These were frontiersmen in buckskin trousers, hunting shirts, moccasins, and hats made of animal skins. They rarely took baths and wore the same clothes until they rotted. When they got a job on a boat, they brought along a straw mattress or a buffalo robe for bedding.[10]

These men's lives were generally short. Some boats had a hearth in the cabin, but most had a sandbox in which the crew built fires on deck. Members of the crew usually did their own cooking and subsisted on bacon, biscuits, coffee, and whiskey, supplementing their diet with game or produce from the riverbanks. A diet lacking in dairy foods and fresh vegetables weakened them. Hard work in icy winters and hot summers lowered their resistance to disease. Lice and vermin flourished on the wooden boats. Lack of sanitation produced bacterial infections, and scourges like yellow fever caused many deaths. Many rivermen, with little or no access to medical care, tried to cure themselves with useless remedies or self-medicated with alcohol.[11]

Historians agree that these early boatmen were a hard-drinking, smoking, tobacco-chewing, cussing, gambling, fighting, and generally unruly bunch of men, who sometimes crossed the line from vice to violent crime. Passengers frequently complained about the men's foul language, tobacco breath, and spitting. Card games went on constantly and sometimes ended in brawls. Rivermen gambled boisterously on the boat and in the towns on shore. Alcohol fueled incidents of violence, and all the boatmen carried knives and guns. In 1819, on the keelboat *Massac* floating above Ste. Genevieve, a drunken crew member named Banks Finch provoked a fight and ended up dead from stab wounds.[12]

The steamboat era brought some changes in the habits and culture of the boatmen. Many rivermen continued to smoke, swear, drink, gamble, and fight, but life on the boats and in river towns became a bit more sedate. Steamboat owners and captains tried to protect their investment by controlling the men's behavior. Passengers demanded safe and comfortable travel. The temperance movement gradually made inroads in the consumption of alcohol in America. In the Mississippi valley, the population grew, and governmental control of people's behavior increased. Cities and towns created police forces and passed ordinances aimed at curbing vice and crime in the waterfront districts. But the river remained an unpredictable and sometimes dangerous place.[13]

A bank robbery, murder, and execution in St. Louis in 1841 revealed yet again the danger that clung to some who chose river life. Madison Henderson, a slave, and three free black men died by hanging on July 9 after confessing to robbing the Pettus Bank, killing two clerks, and setting fire to the building. All four of the men obtained work as hands on steamboats as young adults in the 1830s. One of the free black men, Charles Brown, testified that he helped slaves to board boats heading north to St. Louis on their way to freedom. By 1840, Henderson, Brown, and two other men, James Seward and Amos Warrick, were living in St. Louis and working on the steamer *Agnus.*[14]

Historian Thomas Buchanan has argued that these young black men lived in a world in which crime was accepted as an assertion of freedom. When they found their way to the docks, they joined a workforce that included thousands of free blacks and slaves out of reach of the owners' tight control. Even the slaves lived in circumstances of quasi-freedom. Because of this, riverboat workers became role models for young black boys hoping to find their own way in the world. Brown and the others traveled widely on the Mississippi, Missouri, and Ohio rivers before landing in St. Louis. Like other black boatmen, they collected wages and supplemented them by smuggling goods out of cities like New Orleans and selling them in other places. Henderson and Seward also became habitual thieves.[15]

Joining forces in the summer of 1840, the men entered the Pettus Bank, but discovered that they could not open the safe. Frustrated, they grabbed a small amount of money and then beat two clerks to death before starting the fire. After the robbery, the river men left the city on various boats. A manhunt that spread through several states resulted in the capture of Seward and Henderson in Cairo, Brown in Cincinnati, and Warrick on the Missouri River steamer *Omega*. After the trial, conviction, and execution, enraged citizens of St. Louis mutilated the men's bodies.[16]

Most of the men who worked on steamboats were not thieves or bank robbers, but the world they inhabited was sometimes brutal. In the early months of 1849, a young man named George Forman left his native Canada hoping to strike it rich in the California Gold Rush. After a trip down the Ohio River to Cairo, he observed a "dismal flat" landscape in the Mississippi bottoms. The river water, he said, was "gritty to drink and scours those not used to it." From Cairo, he proceeded up the Mississippi and Missouri rivers and then to the Far West. When his hopes of instant riches failed, he returned to St. Louis and stayed in a boardinghouse on the levee. By April he had found work as a deckhand on the steamer *Sarah* bound for New Orleans. The work was hard, he later wrote, and the mates were cruel.[17]

Forman recalled in an unpublished memoir that he was not a typical deckhand, because he was literate and not a drinker, carouser, or gambler. He and the other hands, he said, worked "night and day with only short spells of sleep." The mates might wake them up at any moment to load or unload freight or bring wood for the furnaces. The men were "fed like pigs out of pans on deck," and they slept in bunks, with every man carrying his own bedding from one steamer to another. The mates "knocked and kicked the men about like brutes." He claimed to have seen many men "knocked overboard with handspikes and abused like dogs."[18]

The young and slight Forman could not carry heavy loads of wood, and so the officers put him ashore at Memphis. He returned to the boat as a passenger and rode down to New Orleans. In May 1849, he took passage on the steamer *Glencoe* and went back to St. Louis. Many German immigrants were passengers on that boat, and some of them died of cholera during the trip. Arriving in St. Louis during the worst period of the epidemic, Forman took up residence in the same boardinghouse where he had stayed before. He helped to carry the bodies of cholera victims down the stairs and credited his own survival to clean living. After this terrible experience, he shipped as a hand on another steamer and went on to have many adventures in North America and Australia.[19]

Rosche learned as a young deck-sweep that not all mates were cruel. After saying good-bye to his family in St. Louis, he returned to the dock and reported for work on the *Adriatic,* a Union transport vessel during the Civil War. He followed a line of soldiers up the gangplank and reported to the mate, who spat tobacco juice into the river and then told him what his job would be. Most important, he would sweep the decks in the early hours of the morning when the passengers were in their cabins. After that he would help the cook by peeling potatoes, emptying the garbage buckets, and carrying wood for the stoves. In addition to these jobs, he would do whatever anyone on the boat asked him to do at any time. If he had any spare time, he would fill the lamps with oil and trim the wicks. The mate on the *Adriatic* was gruff and demanding but not mean.[20]

For young Rosche, the work proved less difficult than the mate initially suggested. On the passage down the river, Rosche had time to explore the boat and visit in the roustabouts' quarters, where he heard tales of Mike Fink, the legendary flatboatman. During the day, he watched the river flow between the densely wooded banks. At night, the lamps were kept low, and the boat was very dark, because it was a troop ship passing through Confederate territory.[21]

Another mate helped Rosche when he was stranded in New Orleans. The *Adriatic* was commissioned for the trip downriver, but not for the return trip. Along with other crew members, Rosche found himself on the wharves looking for work. The seven dollars he had received as wages from the *Adriatic* melted away in a few weeks, and no one seemed interested in hiring a twelve-year-old deckhand. Rosche spent six months living on the streets, working odd jobs, shining shoes or selling paper flowers, hungry, lonesome, and too proud to appeal to his relatives in St. Louis. He worked, played, and fought with other "levee urchins" in a wild city full of gambling dens, brothels, and desperate men. At last, the first mate on one of the riverboats declined to hire him but offered to take him on as a helper in return for food and free passage back to St. Louis. Ten days later he was home again, but he had not lost the desire to work on the river.[22]

Charles Allen Smith, who worked as a deckhand on the *Kate Simmons* in the 1880s, wrote a brief diary that explained the troubles and joys of a boatman's life. Long watches on dark nights and hard work cleaning boilers and repairing rudders in cold and snowy weather did not prevent the twenty-two-year-old Smith from exploring the countryside along the river banks. On November 29, 1885, he finished his work and "went to the bank at half past five o'clock in the evening after supper." About forty miles below Cairo, he and other crew members "took a ramble through the woods." On another similar outing above Memphis, he and his companions "took the yawl went ashore, went hunting found lots of wild geese had lots of fun but killed nothing."[23]

On the return trip, above Memphis, on January 1, 1886, Smith had an adventure that confirmed the continuing wild and violent nature of riverboat life. The *Kate Simmons* encountered a small boat with a cabin. A man onboard the little craft pulled out a pistol and threatened the larger boat's pilot, William (Billy) Hepenistall. As Smith told it, "Billy stopped the engines and ran for his revolver then the man began to row and Billy began to shoot. It was fun." Apparently, there was a woman in the cabin of the smaller craft, and she was "swearing out of a window and the first shot she closed the window and that was the last we saw of her, they rowed for life, when he knew he was out of reach of the revolver he fired one shot with his horse pistol."[24]

When young Smith had his adventures on the Mississippi, the world of the boatmen was undergoing a transformation. After the Civil War, before the railroads caught up with a boom in travel, there was a burst of activity on the river, but it was short-lived. Passengers preferred the speed and relative safety of the trains, and the freight business also deserted the old wooden packet boats with their small carrying capacity. Entrepreneurs invested in steel-hulled towboats and barges that could move large quantities of freight with some degree of efficiency, and river workers adjusted to new conditions that, in many respects, still embraced time-honored ways.[25]

In the modern era of towboats and barges, mates and deckhands shouldered the difficult job of "making tow." Compared to the old floating palaces, towboats were small craft consisting of an engine room, a cabin to house the crew, and a glass-enclosed pilothouse. These small but powerful boats pushed barges containing enough cargo to fill hundreds of railroad cars. The crew "made tow" by fastening these barges together in a way that made it possible for the boat to push them through all the turns of the great river. If the crew did its work properly, the pilot could steer the small towboat and its gigantic system of barges as a single integrated vessel. Reflecting on his work as a towboat captain, Larry Drum praised his mate, Verdell Ledgewood: "All the crew liked him, and he knew how to make tow."[26]

For mates and crew members in the twentieth century, working conditions improved, but the rhythm of work and leisure changed very little. Crews worked intensely for short periods of time, usually about a month, then faced long stretches of idleness. Days and nights on the river were divided into six-hour watches. Bells rang at 5:30 in the morning for breakfast. One group of men bolted their food and was ready to stand watch at 6:00. The men who were relieved of duty then came to breakfast and socialized, rested, or went to sleep. The same sequence of events occurred at 11:30, when the crew had a midday meal, and again at 5:30 for supper. Another meal would be offered before the last watch began at midnight.[27]

Living conditions on the boats changed for the better, but some old habits lingered. Rivermen who lived long enough to remember the old days sometimes became nostalgic about life on the wood-hulled packet boats, despite the fact that those boats were firetraps, and most of them were infested with vermin. Modern steel-hulled boats provided a much higher level of safety and cleanliness. Flush toilets, hot showers, and laundry service made a huge difference in the lives of the crew. Sleeping arrangements improved. Crew members shared rooms, but they slept in regular beds with clean sheets. There was more privacy, but the men still lived together in close quarters, sharing an intense communal life. In the long evenings after supper, deckhands on the towboats would sit on small couches in the wheelhouse and tell stories, just as the rivermen of the past would sit on benches or boards, smoking and joking, near the pilot's wheel.[28]

There were striking continuities and some differences in the kinds of people who worked on the river. With the exception of cooks and maids, the workforce remained overwhelmingly male. Pilots, mates, and engineers were older professional men. Deckhands were usually teenagers or young men, but increasingly they came from the high schools and colleges, not from the wild, ungoverned levees. They were more literate than their predecessors, less likely to drink excessively and get into brawls, and yet they remained a diverse and unpredictable group of people, literate yet ignorant, cultured but crude, reflective but rowdy, ambitious but lazy, cruel but kind, and hard to categorize. The one characteristic they tended to have in common was a disdain for the forty-hour week, the office cubicle, and the tedious aspects of modern life.[29]

Something else, something intangible, a feeling about the river, connected the boatmen past and present. Mark Twain understood this when he sat on the bench watching Bixby guide the boat through treacherous currents. Louis Rosche understood it when, at the age of twelve, he hid inside a steamboat, not knowing what kind of boat it was or where it was going, but determined to go wherever it might take him. Larry Drum knew he had to go "out there" on the river when other young men were going away to college. There was something "out there" that gripped him and would not let go. Boatmen were different from everyone else. People on the banks waved at them and watched them—and envied them. They had escaped from ordinary life, and they had a chance to penetrate the secrets of the great dark, swirling Mississippi. Rivermen felt a strange attachment to their calling. They were proud of who they were, in spite of the fact that they had to show deference to pilots and captains and take orders from, well, seemingly, everyone. The work they did was hard and repetitive; some people might see it as drudgery. But the work was not what called them. It was the river.

The dredge boat *Ste. Genevieve*
From the Collection of the Cape River Heritage Museum, Cape Girardeau

Don Karl of Ste. Genevieve expressed mixed feelings about his long career on the water with the Corps of Engineers. He started as a dishwasher in 1964. For a while he worked as a deckhand for another Ste. Genevieve man, Don Bader, on the dredge boat *Kennedy*. "I was under him," said Karl. "He was the mate on my watch." After that Karl moved up to what he called "the exalted position of first mate." He switched from the *Kennedy* to the *Ste. Genevieve*, another boat belonging to the Corps. He remembered working a six-hour shift, taking a three- or four-hour nap, and then working another six-hour shift every day. He was so tired he never had any trouble sleeping even though his bed was above the noisy engine room.[30]

He was proud of the job he did. "I did well, I guess. However, when I got up to the first mate's position, that was really more than I wanted. I was under the captain, under the office, and then from the lowest deckhand on up everybody's after you. Do this. When are you going to do that?" He had a lot of responsibilities. "I had to really order all the stuff, trash pick-ups on up to getting groceries in.... Every time you turned around it was something else. I think at times it just got a little much. But I guess I was just like an old steer. I gave it a good try. And there was this satisfaction of getting the job done."[31]

Reflecting back on his days on the river he mused, "The sunrise and sunsets were always beautiful," but then he added, "if you could take the time—if you didn't have twenty-five things to do in the next twenty minutes."[32]

Would he do it again? He had no answer to that. But his wife, Ellen, said sometimes she met him on the boat and rode with him for a while, and she remembered the currents, the wind blowing, "so cool. There's nothing like floating on the river."[33]

Her husband had to admit that it was a pretty satisfying thing.[34]

CHAPTER SEVEN

Cape Girardeau, Missouri

The ferryboat *Gladys* at Cape Girardeau
From the Collection of the Cape River Heritage
Museum, Cape Girardeau

We reached the Cape Wednesday afternoon at 1 o'clock and found Capt. A. C. Jaynes' new ferryboat, the *Gladys.* She is the best ferryboat that Cape Girardeau has ever had, and Capt. Jaynes, who built her, is to be congratulated. His son Roy is pilot of her.

—*Waterways Journal,* December 2, 1911

Cape Girardeau, halfway between St. Louis and Memphis, was a busy ferryboat landing from 1806 until 1928, when a highway bridge began carrying traffic across the river to Illinois. The city took its name from a rocky "cape" briefly occupied by a French trader, Jean Girardot, whose surname was spelled in many different ways. Another Frenchman Louis Lorimier, a very successful trader and entrepreneur, was the town's first permanent resident. He also established the area's first ferry, a wooden flatboat, before the age of steam.[1]

Lorimier emigrated from Canada in the late eighteenth century. As a young man, following in his father's footsteps, Lorimier developed a wide network of relationships with the Native Americans of the Ohio and Mississippi valleys. In the 1790s, he settled in Cape Girardeau, where he established a home and trading post on the river and received large land grants from the Spanish government. The Delaware and Shawnee tribes held frequent encampments in the area. Lorimier, who was nearly six feet tall, wore his hair in a very long braid and walked with the quiet steps and erect posture of the Native Americans. His first wife Charlotte, a Native American, had long dark hair and wore bright ornaments. After her death in 1803, Lorimier married a woman named Marie, who was of Native American and French heritage. When he died in 1812, his children inherited a large estate, including great tracts of land, two water-powered flour mills on local creeks, and the ferry service.[2]

In the 1840s, Alexander Giboney and his associates operated a steam-powered ferry on the Mississippi. Giboney's family arrived in Cape Girardeau just a few years after Lorimier established the settlement. The family's patriarch, also named Alexander, died shortly after he came to the area, leaving his widow, Rebecca (Ramsay) Giboney, in charge of his property and a family of four sons and three daughters. The Ramsays and the Giboneys owned large tracts of land and a substantial number of slaves. Rebecca Giboney managed a sizable plantation until her death in 1840. Her granddaughter married the enterprising Louis Houck, who built a majestic home on the Giboneys' land. Alexander was, perhaps, one of the lesser-known members of a distinguished family, but he did help to bring Cape Girardeau into the age of steam.[3]

During the peak years of steamboating, Cape Girardeau's mills and businesses grew rapidly. Large packet boats carrying mail, freight, and passengers stopped regularly to load and unload cargo in this booming little town on the west bank. Farmers from the Ozark hills and the bottomlands of southeastern Missouri brought wagons full of corn, wheat, and cotton to the wharves and stayed to shop in local stores. Steamboat captains became familiar and dashing figures, whether they lived in town or only stopped to visit when their boats were passing through. Local people came to the riverfront to watch the roustabouts carry bales and boxes up and down the gangplanks. Roustabouts gave nicknames to local merchants. For example, the Meyer-Albert Grocer Company became the "Ace of Diamonds." Crew members frequented local bars, pool halls, and boardinghouses. Captains, pilots, and mates became part of the social elite, inviting townspeople to balls and banquets onboard their vessels.[4]

When the Civil War began, Union leaders recognized the importance of Cape Girardeau's location on an accessible slope on the bank of the Mississippi. From July 1861 through August 1865, federal troops occupied the city and imposed martial law. The army set up offices in the Common Pleas Courthouse high on a hill overlooking the river. Soldiers also occupied Camp Strong on the fairgrounds at the southern edge of town. In addition to keeping the river open, the troops kept strict order in the Southern-leaning community. Many citizens, particularly German Americans, supported the Union. Colonel George C. Thilenius headed a local militia unit that supported federal troops. The garrison commander of the occupying force constantly exhorted citizens and soldiers to remain calm and avoid clashes. Tavern-keepers were not allowed to sell alcohol to soldiers or drunkards, and taverns closed at 10:00 pm. A few defiant Rebels were imprisoned in the basement of the courthouse.[5]

In the fall of 1861, General Ulysses S. Grant ordered the fortification of Cape Girardeau. With the aid of some civilians, including prisoners released from the courthouse, soldiers constructed four forts, unimaginatively named A, B, C, and D. Fort A was a small artillery emplacement on the bluff in the northern part of town. Fort B occupied a high point northwest of town, where soldiers could keep an eye on the roads from Perryville to the north and Jackson to the west. Fort C, southwest of the town, commanded a view of the roads from Commerce, Bloomfield, and Gordonville. The most important installation, Fort D, stood on a point overlooking the river at the south end of town. This fort consisted of a central ammunition house and tents surrounded by earthworks and rifle pits.[6]

While Grant and his army relentlessly pushed south along the banks of the Mississippi in 1863, Confederate General John S. Marmaduke and a band of several thousand poorly armed men invaded southeastern Missouri. As soon as Union officers realized what was happening, they moved men from the surrounding areas into the fortifications at Cape

Girardeau. On April 26, in a downpour, General Jo Shelby and General George W. Carter led two columns of Rebels into the city, where they met fierce resistance. For three or four hours, the noise of artillery was constant and terrible. After several charges failed to break Union lines, the two columns of Confederate soldiers retreated to the west and eventually across the line into Arkansas. The battle was indecisive, but Cape Girardeau and its position overlooking the river remained in Union hands.[7]

In the postwar era, an Illinois-born lawyer relocated to Cape Girardeau. He was the aforementioned Louis Houck, who married into the Giboney family and spent three hectic decades buying property, promoting education, and building railroads. Houck's railroads connected the forested wetlands of Missouri's southeastern Bootheel to timber markets in Cape Girardeau and other cities. By the 1920s, intensive lumbering and swamp drainage projects had opened the region to agriculture. Driven northward by boll weevil infestations, Southern farmers, tenants, and sharecroppers settled in southeastern Missouri, planted cotton, and turned Cape Girardeau into a cotton ginning and shipping hub. At the end of his life, Houck settled down to write several well-regarded histories of southeast Missouri.[8]

Competition from the railroads did not bring a sudden or immediate end to steamboat traffic, and riverboat captains remained popular figures in the river city. Even after he abandoned a local woman and went to St. Louis to live with his second wife, "Buck" Leyhe maintained strong connections with the local business community. In 1925, when the *Southeast Missourian* celebrated the opening of its opulent Spanish-style building on Broadway, Leyhe and the steamer *Cape Girardeau* had a starring role in the production. On Friday September 11, with a marching band leading them, local citizens paraded to the levee to greet the boat carrying dozens of distinguished guests from St. Louis. The newspaper reported that "Capt. 'Buck' Leyhe has taken the *Cape Girardeau* out of commission to have it in the pink of condition and everything that money will provide will be offered the guests." Leyhe hired a group of seven female singers known as the Georgia Gibson Serenaders to entertain onboard the boat, which served as a hotel while the visitors remained in Cape Girardeau. Fireworks on the levee on Saturday night capped the two-day celebration.[9]

A close friend of Leyhe's was Samuel Shrodes, who came to Cape Girardeau as a captain with Eagle Packet Company. The Pennsylvania-born

Shrodes began his career as a ship's carpenter. By 1875, he had moved to St. Louis and married Nettie K. Perkitt. The family moved to Cape Girardeau in 1887, and soon after that Nettie died, leaving behind a grieving husband and three young children. The following year, Captain Shrodes married Idella (or Della) Coffer, and in 1889, Nettie's daughter (also named Nettie) passed away at the age of six. The Shrodes family rented an apartment and later a small house not far from the Eagle Packet Company's offices at the corner of Themis and Water streets. From each of these residences, the captain had a view of the river.[10]

Like many captains, Shrodes aspired to be the owner of a boat. He briefly realized his dream when he bought the steamer *Josie* from the Eagle Packet Company. He continued to work for the company, but this boat belonged to him. Unfortunately, in 1901, the *Josie* became entangled with another boat, and both of them burned. Despite this loss, he continued his life on the river until 1921, when he became ill. He never recovered his health, and when he died in 1924, at the age of seventy-two, the newspaper called him a "Pioneer River Captain." His second wife, Della, passed away in 1930. She, the captain, his first wife, Nettie, and little Nettie, who had died so young, were buried in close proximity in Fairmount Cemetery.[11]

Another close associate of Leyhe was Irvin Albert, whose family had a long-standing connection with Cape Girardeau and the river. Born in 1876, Albert was fascinated by steamboats. When Albert was growing up, his father, Sebastian, owned a boat store that had been established in 1838 at the corner of Water and Themis streets, where the Eagle Packet Company would later have offices. In the early twentieth century, George Meyer came from St. Louis, went into partnership with the Albert family, and opened a new store, the Meyer-Albert Grocer Company, on Main Street. Irvin Albert became an agent for the Eagle Packet Company and continued to operate the Albert Boat Store in the original location. He never married and lived most of his adult life in the home of his sister and her husband. In 1918, when the city council established a port authority, Irvin became the first port warden, whose responsibilities included collecting docking fees, overseeing the operation of the port, and ensuring public safety in the port. After his untimely death in 1923, his younger brother Lee took over the business.[12]

In addition to running their grocery and boat stores, Irvin and his brothers served as official river observers for the U.S. Weather Bureau. Irvin's eldest brother began this work in 1880 and continued until his

**The Albert-Meyer Store near the riverfront
From the Collection of the Cape River Heritage
Museum, Cape Girardeau**

untimely death. Irvin shouldered this responsibility until he too passed away. His younger brother Lee inherited the task and barely missed a day in more than forty years. In the 1920s, Lee Albert made daily trips to the riverfront to measure the water level and post his readings for passing boats. He also recorded the amount of rainfall in the city. Because of his advance warnings, residents of the city could evacuate or take precautions during floods. As time went on, technological innovations made his work easier and more accurate. By the time he retired from this post in 1969, he could determine the level of the river from a gauge in his home.[13]

Not all the businessmen on the riverfront had long histories in Cape Girardeau or connections to old local families. Lee Don, who was born in China around 1870, came to California with his parents when he was about nineteen years old. At this time, many Chinese immigrants found their way to the Mississippi River valley, and many of them settled in St. Louis, where they opened laundries, stores, and restaurants on the riverfront. Lee Don got married in San Francisco but left his wife and children behind when he moved to Missouri around 1904. His parents, wife, and children moved back to China in 1905, and he did not see them again for fifteen years. Between 1905 and 1920, he owned and operated Cape Girardeau's City Laundry at 306 Broadway, a few blocks up the hill from the river.[14]

During the early years of his business, he had two Chinese helpers who lived in the same building where he lived and had his business. In later years, he lived alone but hired women to help him. On June 9, 1920, the *Southeast Missourian* reported that Don was preparing to leave for St. Louis with the intention of returning to China. The paper commented that he had "done a good business. He has been a law-abiding resident for the 15 years he has lived here, and in matters of public interest he has always been a generous contributor of money." Ten days later, the newspaper reported that he was dismantling his shop and planning to sell his laundry machinery.[15]

After visiting friends in St. Louis, he said he wanted to go home to the place where he was born. "When he arrives in China," according to the newspaper, "and is united with his family the one thing that he will indulge in, and the thing that he has been craving for so long a time will be a rest and a nice long vacation." He said he might return to America in a year or two and go back into business but not the laundry business. He was not sorry to leave that behind. "It is the friends whom he has made during the last 15 years that he regrets leaving," the newspaper noted, "those whom he has gained through his honesty in business transactions, his courtesy and service, friends who are cherished to his memory."[16]

Another enterprise that persisted in Cape Girardeau in the late nineteenth and early twentieth centuries was the ferryboat business. A. C. Jaynes and his sons Finis and Roy were the last ferrymen to take vehicles and passengers across the river from Cape Girardeau to the Illinois side. The boat that Roy piloted was named after his sister Gladys. Roy, who was born in 1888, spent most of his working life on the river. While piloting the *Gladys* he helped rescue people from floods and witnessed the disappearance of a towboat in heavy winds. After the opening of a highway bridge in 1928, there was no more demand for the ferry.[17]

The ferry went out of business, and the Jaynes family tried many ways to make a living. In 1930, Roy was piloting a barge for the Marquette Cement Company when he discovered the body of James Romine, a twenty-one-year-old man, who had drowned when his small boat capsized. Roy and a coworker secured a light skiff and brought the body to shore. Roy passed away in 1941 at the age of fifty-four.[18]

Cape Girardeau's business community put its heart and soul into the highway bridge, welcoming the era of the automobile. The local chamber of commerce appointed a bridge committee, obtained the support of state highway officials, and proposed a bill to Congress. In 1926, President Calvin Coolidge signed the Cape Girardeau Bridge Bill, but the bill did not allocate any funding. In one five-day period, 150 volunteers sold more than $500,000 worth of stock certificates to finance the bridge. Many residents, including African Americans, bought stock in the bridge, believing that the project would boost the local economy.[19]

The terrible spring flood of 1927 that caused destruction in the Mississippi River valley did not stop construction of the bridge. Even in the worst days of the flood, workers continued to prepare approaches to the bridge in areas unaffected by high water. When the flood subsided work resumed on concrete piers, the concreted floor of the bridge, and the metal superstructure. On August 22, 1928, lightning struck an eighteen-year-old worker on the bridge. He recovered, but the next day a member of the construction crew fell into the river and drowned. A fisherman on the Illinois side found his body a week later. On August 23, the day of the drowning, the superintendent of the construction company drove the first automobile across the bridge. In September, the bridge opened to great fanfare and celebration.[20]

Bridge promoters did not anticipate the stock market crash of 1929 or the Great Depression of the 1930s. Highway work on the Illinois side of the bridge languished for the next five years, and traffic did not meet estimated levels. Revenue from tolls was very disappointing. Loans went unpaid. In 1935, an Ohio company bought the bridge for $850,000, much less than the cost of construction. Many local investors lost their money. Eventually, toll revenues improved, but floods in 1943 and 1944 forced the bridge to close for short periods of time. The City of Cape Girardeau purchased the bridge in 1946, eventually paid off the debts, and made the bridge toll-free in 1957. Despite the early setbacks, the bridge did eventually live up to its promise of boosting the city's economy.[21]

Near the end of his long life, Lee Albert reflected on the relationship of Cape Girardeau and the Mississippi. He remembered the days when people would sit out on the levee, watching the steamboats gliding by and listening to the calliopes playing. He recalled taking short excursions to the nearby town of Commerce on the *Cape Girardeau* with Captain Buck Leyhe. In Albert's memory, the riverfront was a place of music and romance. After dancing all night, he and his friends would walk along Water Street and "wait for the sun to peep over the willow trees on the Illinois shore and shine on the river." He remembered when A. C. Jaynes watched the construction crews working on the highway bridge and knew his ferry business was doomed. Like a lot of river people, Albert was philosophical about bad weather, hard times, and floods. When asked what he had learned from half a century of close observation of weather and water levels, he repeated what someone had told him very long ago: "When you have lots of rain, you have lots of river."[22]

CHAPTER EIGHT

Stewards, Cooks, and Maids

Charlie Clay as chef on the *Golden Eagle*
From the Collections of the St. Louis Mercantile Library at the University of Missouri–St. Louis

Sometimes they were in mid-river when the breakfast bell sounded; sometimes tied to a landing. The view might be plantation, woods, or small town—it was all one to the *Cotton Blossom* company, intent on coffee and bacon.

—Edna Ferber, *Show Boat*

Riverboats were homes for officers and crew members and hotels for passengers. Cooks, stewards, and maids provided nourishment, creature comforts, and in the best of circumstances, the warmth of a surrogate family for sojourners on a long and treacherous river. Some of the people onboard were haughty "swells"; some were rough adventurers; and in the decades before the Civil War, some of them were slaves.

Before he escaped from slavery in the 1830s, William Wells Brown worked as a waiter, barber, and steward's assistant on several steamboats. As a young man in his teens, Brown had three different masters in St. Louis who lent him out for service on the river. When the steamer *Enterprise* was docked in the city, he heard Senator Thomas Hart Benton deliver a Fourth of July address on the subject of man's inalienable rights. In stark contrast, while Brown was employed on the *Enterprise*, he encountered James Walker, a slave trader, who took note of Brown's efficiency and demeanor. Early in 1832, the young Brown's master hired him out to the slave trader for a year as a custodian of slaves being sent down the Mississippi River.[1]

Brown later described his experiences going south from St. Louis to New Orleans with the slave trader. When they reached one of the stops on the way, Brown wrote, he had to make the old men look younger by shaving off their whiskers and blackening their gray hairs. In New Orleans, Walker forced him to place the slaves on exhibit in a yard (or slave pen) and make them dance and sing for prospective buyers. On one terrible occasion, Brown recalled, Walker snatched a crying baby from its mother and gave the infant to a lady as a gift. In another instance, Walker took another woman's blind child and sold him to an innkeeper for a dollar. During these trips with Walker, Brown learned the true horrors of slavery. Later in his life, he used this knowledge to become a renowned antislavery speaker and writer.[2]

In his novel *Clotel, or The President's Daughter*, Brown created a fictional incident, based on his memories, that captured a sense of life on a river steamer in the time of slavery. As he recalled, many passengers gambled and some lost everything on long nights on the Mississippi. In his story, a passenger named Smith ordered the steward to go call his "boy." A few minutes later, a boy named Jerry was standing on top of the table with silver dollars and bank notes at his feet. Smith lost the game and relinquished the boy to a man named Johnson, who told him to get up in the morning and brush his clothes and clean his boots. The young slave complied, with tears in his eyes.[3]

Another man who worked in various housekeeping functions on the river and later won fame as a writer was John Henton Carter, whose pen name was Commodore Rollingpin. Born in Marietta, Ohio, in 1832, Carter went to work in the galley of a flatboat as a young boy. From the 1840s through the 1860s, he served as a pantry boy, pastry cook, and steward on a variety of riverboats plying the Ohio and Mississippi rivers. By 1870 he had settled in St. Louis, where he became a popular journalist, lecturer, and local character. Literary historian Alexander DeMenil wrote that Carter sometimes went out in public in elegant clothes and sometimes in the rags of a tramp. Despite his eccentricities, he won the respect of many writers and journalists, including Mark Twain. His best-known work, *Commodore Rollingpin's Illustrated Almanac*, included weather predictions, proverbs, short didactic tales, and advertisements for Carter's lectures.[4]

Although he had never been a pilot himself, Carter wrote a series of fictional character sketches from the point of view of a riverboat pilot and published them in 1898 under the title *The Man at the Wheel.* While Carter's writing tended to be sentimental or broadly humorous, one of the sketches told a chilling story of racial hatred and violence. The pilot/narrator began by praising Bill Smith, a free black man who started out as a barber and then set up a gambling business on a flatboat. When Smith made too much money, a group of white gamblers became envious and threatened to burn his boat. Smith faced them down, and they went away, but they came back later, drunk and bloodthirsty, shooting and setting his boat on fire. "You may kill me, you white-livered cowards," said Smith, "but you can't conquer me." To escape the flames, he jumped into the river and was never seen again.[5]

Carter captured the essence of the worn-out but still irascible riverboat mate in his portrait of Jerry Walsh. In this little tale, Walsh walks into a doctor's office and describes his symptoms. His liver and kidneys are giving him trouble, but that is just the beginning. He takes out a list of the things he needs, including new teeth, a glass eye, three fingers and a thumb on one hand, a wooden leg, three toes on one foot, a new pair of ears, a right hand, some new ribs, and a wig. When the doctor comments that he must have had a rough life, Walsh concedes that he has been struggling since he was three years old. But on the other hand, he boasts, "I've chawed off more ears and noses an' caved in more ribs 'an any man 'at ever follered the Mississippi."[6]

In a more sentimental vein, Carter wrote about a longtime deckhand named Jim Wright. He never aspired to any other position, but he took great pride in stowing freight and keeping the decks in order. If a rouster stole whiskey from a barrel, Jim would take quick and decisive action. He seemed to think he was responsible for anything that went wrong on the boat. But he did not want any thanks for it. He wanted only one thing. When he died, he wanted the flags lowered to half-mast, but it so happened that when he did pass away on a riverboat, his crewmates forgot to lower the flags. They took his body out to a high bluff to bury it, and just as they were about to put the cover on the coffin, he sat up and asked about the flags. The men had to admit their error of omission. "Jim looked as if he had lost his last friend. His heart was broken, and he said he didn't want to live any longer." After a few awkward moments, he lay back down and told them to go on with his funeral.[7]

For stewards, cooks, maids, and cabin boys, life was just as difficult as it was for mates and deckhands. On the old steamers, cabin and kitchen crews sometimes had to work eighteen hours a day. Chores were seemingly endless. Cabin boys scoured knives, washed basins, kept up fires, filled water barrels, fetched and carried, and helped keep the boat clean. Cooks worked in hot steamy kitchens located in front of the wheelhouse. Behind the kitchen was the washhouse. On the big floating palaces, there might be a fine and varied menu for passengers and officers. Cabin workers had the advantage of access to the leftovers. For crew members, on many boats, the staple foods were meat, hardtack, boiled potatoes, and black coffee. Cooks and other members of the cabin crew often took up bad habits like drinking, smoking, and chewing tobacco. Tobacco juice and sweat sometimes found their way into the food.[8]

Like all officers and crew members, cooks faced the dangers of icy water, perilous currents, and volatile machinery. In October 1902, a disaster occurred on the St. Louis-based towboat *Fred Nellis* on its way upriver to Thebes, Illinois. Mrs. Frank Hill, the engineer's wife, was cooking breakfast on the boat when the boiler exploded, wrecking the upper part of the vessel. The blast killed two people—Mrs. Hill and the second engineer—and wounded several others. Frank Hill was slightly scalded. The Hills' five children, who were living in a house on the barge connected to the towboat, survived the disaster. The eldest of them was twelve, and the youngest was under two years old.[9]

In rare instances, a cook received special recognition for his or her skills. In 1909, the Diamond Jo Line, operating between St. Louis and St. Paul, sent a young black man named Charlie Clay to cook for President William Howard Taft when he made an inspection tour of the Mississippi River from Keokuk, Iowa, to Memphis. Taft and his party rode on the flagship of a sixteen-ship flotilla. His trip made an especially vivid impression on people in Cape Girardeau, where he disembarked and gave a speech. Huge crowds came to the riverfront in the early-morning hours of October 26 to witness the docking of the presidential vessel. He was the first president to visit Cape Girardeau, and people celebrated the event for years as Taft Day.[10]

When Clay cooked for the presidential entourage, he was only about eighteen years old. Born in Mississippi in 1891, he later settled in St. Louis with his wife, Alice. From census records it appears the couple had no children. In 1930, he apparently had left the steamboat business and worked as a cook in a railroad dining car. A few years later he returned to the river and went to work for the Eagle Packet Company, serving as a chef on the *Golden Eagle* and the *Cape Girardeau*. He continued to serve on the same boat in the 1940s, when the *Cape Girardeau* became the *Gordon C. Greene*.[11]

As passenger service faded away and towboats replaced steamboats, cooks and servers continued to play an important role in life on the river. On some of the large dredge boats, with crews of more than fifty men, six or more people worked in the galley. As first mate Don Karl recalled, on these large boats, a cook, a second cook, a night cook, a baker, and two waiters would prepare and serve meals at six in the morning, noon, six in the evening, and midnight. The night cook would peel all the potatoes for the next day and serve the midnight meal and the breakfast. Karl remembered a pilot named Cletis Pierre Menard, who went to bed every night at eight, because he was finished working for the day. But when he smelled the bacon cooking for the men who started their shift at midnight, he would come out and have a sandwich. Karl believed that a good galley was essential to the operation of the boat: "Without it, you would have had insurrection all the time."[12]

Some dredge boats and barge lines continued the tradition of hiring male stewards and cooks, but more and more women came onboard, as twentieth-century innovations changed the lives of housekeeping crews. Modern appliances and higher standards of cleanliness gradually transformed boat kitchens into bright and inviting spaces for socializing as well as cooking. In off hours, deckhands offered to help with food preparation and clean-up, partly to relieve their boredom, and partly to joke and flirt with members of the opposite sex. Serious gambling diminished as a part of life on the boats, but friendly card games went on for hours at kitchen tables.[13]

In the 1940s Edwin and Louise Rosskam asked women why they went to work on towboats. One attraction, of course, was the relatively good pay, compared with similar jobs in river towns. Cooks were considered officers on the boats, and maids were paid the same amount as deckhands. In many cases, the women had grown up near the river and longed to see what it was like "out there." Some had fathers and brothers who worked on the boats. Typically, they cooked or served food in restaurants frequented by rivermen. Someone offered them jobs on the river, and they took them. If they could cope with homesickness, they stayed.[14]

Men and women on the towboats created their own social life. Cooks and maids spent warm evenings sitting on benches on the deck, watching the river go by and reading magazines. They arranged each other's hair and had long, slow conversations. Men and women mingled in the kitchen and the crew's lounge, smoking cigarettes, telling stories, and drinking coffee. Older women became maternal figures to the young deckhands and maids. Women shared cabins with other women; there was strict gender separation in sleeping arrangements. Naturally, there were courtships, elopements, and love affairs, but married couples rarely worked together on boats; many employers would not allow it.[15]

The towboat *Missouri*
From the Collection of the Cape River Heritage Museum, Cape Girardeau

In general, riverboat crews recognized the importance of their cooks and gave them special consideration. Captain Larry Drum said the men on his towboats showed great respect to the female members of his team. If a woman was a good cook, the men would treat her with reverence. They would take out the trash and help set the table, because they wanted her to stay. Poor cooks did not last long, according to Drum, but good ones deserved and commanded respect. Captain Buck Leyhe had also known the value of a good cook. The *Waterways Journal* quoted him as saying that the cook was more important than a captain on a riverboat. "You can't keep a good pilot, no matter what you pay him, unless you feed him to his satisfaction. And believe me, river pilots know good food."[16]

Rose Marie Thrower went to work as a cook on a towboat in 1979 because she needed to support her children. She was working in a girls' dormitory in Cape Girardeau when a friend told her about openings with the Missouri Barge Line. As she remembered, "He told me to come into the office, and I did, and so the next trip out I was on the boat." On that trip she went from St. Paul, Minnesota, to Houston, Texas, in thirty days. "I cried for thirty days," she said. "A lot of salty food."[17]

More than thirty years later, she reflected on her experience on Mississippi River barges from the late 1970s to the early 1990s. Generally, she said, there would be ten people on the boat, seven or eight deckhands, a mate, a captain, a pilot, and a cook. On some trips, there was also a maid to do the cleaning. Everyone got along well: "they better get along with me or they wouldn't have food. They called me the 'captain'. They were good to me." Often she was the only woman on the boat, but the men did not take advantage of her. "They knew better than to get out of line, because the first mate was always around to make sure they stayed like they were supposed to, and if they didn't the captain got hold of them."[18]

Walter Scott, the captain on the *Elizabeth Ann*, advised her to transfer to a different company. "He said, Rose, if you're going to stay out here, what you need to do is transfer over to Agri-Trans, because they pay much more." So she went to St. Louis for an interview, "and by George, they just put me right on. They paid about three times as much as the college where I was working in the dormitory." She worked on a boat called the *White Dawn*, and later she worked on the *Vanguard*, making six trips a year. She would be on the river for thirty days and off for thirty days.[19]

When she was out on the river, she had to be up early. "Breakfast had to be at five, five-thirty." It was a big breakfast of "home-made (boat-made) biscuits, sausage, bacon, sometimes ham, gravy, eggs, any way they wanted them." She baked bread nearly every day, and "every day I made bread I made cinnamon rolls." She would make a batch of bread dough and divide it in half. Half of it would be for dinner rolls, and the other half would be cinnamon rolls.[20]

The meals were hearty. "Sunday was fried chicken.... Monday was beef or pork roast with mashed potatoes and gravy with different vegetables and homemade bread." Grocery orders were large. "Every two weeks," she said, "we'd stock up with a thousand dollars in groceries. Anything anybody wanted." She or the captain would fill out the order form from the boat store, "and then when we got close, they'd bring it out to our boat."[21]

She had a big kitchen with modern appliances, "everything a person could want, dishwasher, garbage disposal, Kitchen-Aid mixer." There were about four dining tables and steam tables for keeping the food warm while crew members served themselves. A refrigerator with a glass door held condiments and drinks. No one ever had to go hungry. "If they didn't want a full cooked meal, they had stuff that they could fix themselves. And they did—a lot."[22]

The life could be lonely, but crew members kept each other company on the boat and in towns along the river. Sometimes Rose and the maid would get off the boat and go shopping. She remembered one evening in Joliet, Illinois: "One of the deckhands' sister lived there, and the captain let me an him go and meet her at the lock, and we went out to a movie, *The Black Stallion*." But she missed her children. That was the worst part of the job. On the day she first went out on the boat, two of her sons were scheduled to graduate from high school that night. But, she said, she had to go. She tried to be home for holidays. "I think I was out there one Christmas. The rest of the time, one way or another, I managed to be home."[23]

She did what she had to do to help her family, and she looked back with pride at her life on the river. During an interview she paged through scrapbooks filled with pictures of boats. Three of her sons stopped by to chat. Each time that happened, she would look up and say, "That's one of mine." Her daughter, Tammi Pettet, sat with her and prompted her to talk about her experiences. She had worked on the river for fifteen years. "Half of this would be at home, and half would be on the boat. And then

Rose Thrower
Photograph courtesy of Rose Thrower and Tammi Pettet

when she [Tammi] was getting ready to have Drake [Rose's grandson], I quit." She had missed part of the years when her children were growing up, and she did not want to miss the time with her grandchild.[24]

Cooks, stewards, and maids did what they could to bring the comforts of home to passengers and crew members on steamboats and towboats. People went out on the river for all kinds of reasons and brought all kinds of baggage—physical, social, and psychological—along with them when they came onboard. Bonds formed among crew members in their sleeping quarters and around the kitchen table. River life, with all its dangers, had a beauty of its own. But life on the river was never completely removed from life on the land.

CHAPTER NINE

Cairo, Illinois

The Cairo levee
From the Collections of the St. Louis Mercantile Library
at the University of Missouri–St. Louis

Cairo has a heavy railroad and river trade, and her situation at the junction of the two great rivers is so advantageous that she cannot well help prospering.

—Mark Twain, *Life on the Mississippi*

Cairo's greatest advantage, its position at the confluence of the Ohio and Mississippi rivers, also contributed to its ruin. From the very beginning, despite predictions of inevitable glory, Cairo struggled to stay alive. During the Civil War, the city became a center of military activity, but postwar optimism soon gave way to disappointment. In the era of Reconstruction, the city developed a culture of segregation that led, in the twentieth century, to a long and costly battle over civil rights. Failed enterprises, dashed hopes, and racial conflict formed the terrible burden of Cairo's history, but a long series of disastrous floods helped to drag the city down.[1]

In 1817, when the first steamboat blew its whistle on the Mississippi, a Baltimore businessman named John G. Comegys sent scouts to survey the swampy, heavily forested land around the great junction of two rivers. Impressed with the area's potential, he purchased 1,800 acres of bottomland. It was Comegys who selected the name "Cairo," invoking the grandeur of ancient Egypt. Early in 1818, he obtained a charter for the City and Bank of Cairo, but he died soon after, and his ambitious enterprise failed, although other men attempted to make Cairo a great and prosperous city.[2]

During the steamboat era, the city enjoyed intermittent flurries of activity. Some local merchants operated from boats tied up at the wharf; others sold goods from small vessels that traveled from place to place. Larger riverboats sometimes stopped, but often ice, low water, or a lack of passengers caused them to bypass Cairo. Sales of local property were sluggish, and population grew very slowly. There were signs of prosperity after 1855, but the flood of 1858 discouraged new settlers. By 1860, the city's population was only slightly more than two thousand people, of whom about fifty were African American. Many of the white residents were Southern sympathizers.[3]

Cairo's population increased dramatically during the Civil War, when the city played a crucial role in the Union's effort to control the Mississippi. The small, struggling city became hugely important as a military base and center for the purchase, conversion, construction, and servicing of gunboats and the recruitment of manpower for both the army and the navy. In August of 1861, three Union gunboats, *Tyler*, *Conestoga*, and *Lexington*, all of which were side-wheelers armed for war, arrived in Cairo as the vanguard of an immense fleet. As they approached the town, crew members saw blue-jacketed army pickets on the stone levees, rough-looking wooden barracks, tents on the west bank of the river at Bird's Point, and earthworks stretching across the muddy landscape. Cairo, with its unpaved streets, open sewers, and plank sidewalks, had already become an armed camp as well as a haven for outlaws, ruffians, and Rebel spies.[4]

The exigencies of war improved Cairo's economy but aggravated its social problems. With an urgent need for naval manpower, the Union recruited hardened old river pilots and deckhands for military service. Traditional navy officers, whose only experience was on the sea, relied on the expertise of these seasoned rivermen. Drunkenness, violence, and thievery were persistent problems among these men, and military justice was swift and severe. Cairo's general population could also be unruly, and Union officers imposed martial law to cut down on gambling and prostitution. During the early months of the war, the port was closed, and businesses suffered, but by 1862, river trade had resumed, and the city's economy improved greatly. Grant set up his headquarters at the St. Charles Hotel near the railroad depot on Second Street. Nearly all the supplies for the Vicksburg campaign passed through Cairo.[5]

The Union's naval campaign suffered a temporary setback when tragedy struck the steamer *Ruth* just six miles downstream from Cairo. Late in the evening on August 4, 1863, the *Ruth* stopped in Cairo to refuel. Just before midnight, fire broke out between the decks. Captain Ben Pegram ran the ship at full speed to the Missouri shore, where passengers and crew ran for their lives. Twenty-six people, including five soldiers, the paymaster, and two clerks, failed to escape. The blaze continued for six hours, completely destroying the vessel, which had been carrying more than two million dollars in paper currency to pay the soldiers in Grant's army. After the wreckage cooled, searchers recovered a safe, but they found only tiny fragments of the money.[6]

During the last few years of the war, the Union recruited free African Americans and runaway slaves for the army and navy. Officers farther south sent "contraband" (escaped and captured slaves) to Cairo for enlistment on gunboats. For example, in the fall of 1862, officers of the *Black Hawk* recruited a former enslaved farmhand named John Jackson as a "coal heaver," who helped to fuel the boilers. Many black men signed on as laborers, carpenters, cooks, and stewards. Typically, African American deckhands worked in all-black work parties, slept in hammocks, and ate their meals on deck. Among the tasks assigned to them were cleaning decks, wiping guns, and pumping water out of the holds.[7]

Throughout the war, black men and women found their way onto the *Red Rover,* the first hospital ship in U.S. history. The boat had begun its life as a commercial steamer and then become a kind of floating barracks for the Confederacy. Abandoned by the Rebels after the Battle of Island Number 10, the boat fell into Union hands. After extensive renovations, in June 1862, the vessel entered the federal gunboat service at Cairo. From then until the end of the war, the *Red Rover* carried enough medical supplies, provisions, and crew members to serve up to two hundred sick and disabled men. Runaway slaves, including both men and women, joined the crew in many capacities. Most women worked as laundresses, although some achieved the rank of nurses. Men worked as laborers, seamen, and also as nurses; in fact, more men than women were employed in caring for patients.[8]

At the end of the war, some African American veterans mustered out in Cairo, where they began to build new lives. In 1863, a former slave named Violet Crawford found refuge on a flatboat and then in a contraband camp near Cairo. Eventually, she was able to move into an apartment with a woman friend. At that time she met George Washington, a black crew member on the tugboat *Myrtle,* which serviced the gunboats at Cairo. He courted her during the time he spent on shore, and in 1867 they married. The couple spent the rest of their lives in Cairo, eventually raising a family. Cairo acquired many such residents during the war, people who stayed and made new lives for themselves. At the end of the war, the city's population had grown to more than eight thousand, of which two thousand were black.[9]

In the late 1860s, Cairo seemed poised to become a hub of railroad and river transportation. Emblematic of the city's high hopes was the Custom House, an imposing and elegant building designed by Alfred B. Mullett. Construction began in 1867, and the building opened in 1872 as a collection point for duties on imports traveling upriver from New Orleans. Over the years, as river traffic declined and railroads bypassed the city, the building housed a post office, courtrooms, and various government offices before falling into complete disuse in 1975.[10]

Through the late 1870s and early 1880s, high hopes once again fell to hard knocks. Spring floods damaged the levees year after year. Stagnant water and drainage problems made the waterfront a breeding place for mosquitoes that carried yellow fever during the epidemic of 1878. By September of that year, with fear spreading upriver from Memphis, one third of Cairo's population had fled the city. Among those who remained, there were about one hundred cases of the fever, resulting in fifty deaths. During a terrible freeze in the winter of 1881, teams of men with axes tried to chop through the ice. In the face of all these difficulties, optimism began to fade.[11]

A persistent problem for the city, into the early twentieth century, was its widespread reputation as a wide-open town, known for vice, crime, and lawlessness. Young Charlie Metheny (born in 1901) worked as a delivery boy and delivered telegrams to the local brothels. Many of these messages came from rivermen, who wanted to make reservations for services when they arrived in town. Years later, Metheny told a reporter for the *New York Times* that many of the houses of prostitution were on Thirteenth Street, but those were the less prestigious addresses, where deckhands could afford to go. Other bordellos on Eighteenth Street served mates, pilots, and captains.[12]

Liquor, gambling, and prostitution provided some of the most stable sources of revenue for the local government, which sold liquor licenses and collected fines from drunkards and ladies of the night. Despite the city's periodic efforts at reform, saloons, brothels, and gambling dens flourished. Pickpockets, thieves, and vagrants congregated around these establishments. A 1905 investigation showed that much of the city's crime originated in the "low dives" that operated under state liquor licenses, but local authorities rarely took take action, even when crime became violent. In 1907, four murders went unpunished, causing terrible discontent among the citizenry.[13]

The city's raw edge became visible to the wider world in 1909 when the rape and murder of Mary Pelley led to the lynching of two men, one black and one white. Pelley, a young, white salesclerk took the streetcar home from work on Monday, November 8. Early the next morning, a child discovered her bruised body in an alley. By nightfall, police had arrested five suspects, all of whom were black, including William "Froggie" James. Throughout the night, mobs formed and dispersed at police headquarters and James's house. The next day, the sheriff and a deputy took James out of town into a rural wooded area. A mob followed, took custody of James, and brought him back to Cairo by train. That night, in downtown Cairo on a well-lighted street, a crowd watched as furious vigilantes first attempted to hang James and then, failing at that, riddled his body with five hundred bullets. Still crazed, the mob went to the courthouse and seized Henry Salzner, a white man who was charged with killing his wife, dragged him out into the street and hanged and then shot him. On November 11, the Illinois National Guard restored order to Cairo.[14]

Social problems surely contributed to Cairo's failure to prosper, but constant flooding sealed its fate. Back-to-back disasters in 1912 and 1913 convinced railroad developers and industrialists to find other, less problematic locations. In the spring of 1912, surging water covered lumber yards, factories, telephone wires, and the arms of telephone poles. Railroad embankments were severely damaged, and Cairo became an island, cut off from railroad lines on every side. Before the city had a chance to rebuild, the flood of 1913 covered low-lying areas, although damage to the city was relatively minor. In subsequent years, the community made sporadic efforts to improve and maintain its levees, but seepage (water coming up from the ground) remained a problem, and the city was always vulnerable to the next big flood.[15]

In the spring of 1927, both the Ohio and the Mississippi rivers overflowed, causing one of the worst calamities in U.S. history. During this flood, the dikes broke at Dorena, Missouri, north of New Madrid. Below this point, river waters covered much of the lowlands from Cairo to the Gulf of Mexico. The flood caused distress in seven states, including Missouri and Illinois, doing its worst damage in Mississippi, Arkansas, and Louisiana. In the aftermath of the flood, the Corps, the American Red Cross, and other agencies responded with a truly heroic campaign to give shelter and distribute food to victims. The army provided boats, equipment, and quarters for Red Cross volunteers, Coast Guard rescue teams, relief workers, and refugees. After the flood, the Corps made plans to avert a similar catastrophe. Unfortunately, as we will see, the flood-control measures that saved Cairo caused serious problems on the Missouri side of the river.[16]

The next catastrophe to hit Cairo was the Great Depression. In the 1930s, the city's basic industries, including lumber, collapsed, and unemployment rose dramatically. By 1935, nearly half of Cairo's population received public assistance (then known as "relief"). When other localities began to recover from the Depression, Cairo continued to stagnate. During World War II, military bases and defense plants brought jobs and dollars to other communities, but not to Cairo. The 1950 census revealed that the city had lost more than two thousand residents in the previous ten years, reducing the total population to about fourteen thousand, as young men and women left Cairo to search for opportunities elsewhere. It became a self-perpetuating cycle. Employers declined to open plants in the city partly due to the lack of a youthful workforce.[17]

Throughout the 1950s, Cairo struggled economically, and by 1961 the federal government had identified it as a distressed area, troubled by persistent unemployment. Between 1950 and 1960, the city's population again declined dramatically to about nine thousand residents, of whom 62 percent were white, and 38 percent were black. The lumber, railroad, and river industries showed no signs of reviving. Federal government programs provided some assistance, including low-cost housing, but private enterprises repeatedly failed. Cairo's enduring reputation as a wide-open town attracted some business but overall had a depressing effect on the economy. Sociologists noted that the seemingly endless cycle of failure, unemployment, vice, and lawlessness resulted in many residents struggling with a psychological state of frustration, resignation, and despair.[18]

Black citizens of Cairo suffered not only poverty and hopelessness but also segregation. Marva Nelson, who grew up in a rural area near Cairo, remembered rude and contemptuous looks from store owners when her family came to town to shop. There were restaurants she could not enter. Most of all she remembered the swimming pool with its clean blue water. The children in her neighborhood swam in muddy drainage ditches full of twigs and trash. The city had opened the pool in 1963, but faced with integration requirements, Cairo quickly closed it and filled it with concrete rather than allow black people to swim in it.[19]

Black residents faced more than such insults. They feared for their lives. On July 15, 1967, Robert L. Hunt, a black soldier on leave, died in the Cairo Police Station. Members of the police department alleged that he had hanged himself with an undershirt, but friends said he was not wearing an undershirt because of the hot, humid weather. There was no inquest until two months after his death, and many people believed he had died as a result of police brutality, and emotions ran high. Riots, fires, and gunshots continued for four days after the young man's death. The mayor and other city officials managed to restore order by promising to end racial discrimination in the police and fire departments and other municipal agencies. They failed to keep their promises, and the struggle for civil rights in Cairo continued for the next six years.[20]

In the aftermath of Hunt's death and the violent public reaction to it, white vigilantes repeatedly harassed black citizens as civil rights groups became more active. A young man named Preston Ewing Jr., president of the local NAACP, lodged official complaints about discrimination in employment. Cairo sometimes took on the appearance of a war zone. On March 31, 1969, white militants engaged in a gun battle with residents of Pyramid Court, a local housing project. Similar battles broke out periodically over the next several years. In response to this violence, local black organizations joined together and formed the United Front of Cairo. Within a week of its founding, the United Front had organized a boycott of white businesses in the city.[21]

Young and old people, men and women, filled St. Columba Church for sermons, songs, and rallies that turned into marches. Reverend Charles Koen presided over many of the meetings, and Hernean Mallory played piano for the United Front choir. Nationally known leaders like Jesse Jackson came to town and participated in demonstrations. There were rallies every Saturday and picket lines every day, and there were also counter-protests, violent incidents, frequent gunshots, and confrontations with police. The demonstrations and boycotts went on day after day, month after month, as Ewing documented the movement with his camera.[22]

J. Anthony Lukas, a writer for the *New York Times*, spent time in Cairo in December of 1970. He heard Reverend Koen preach a stirring sermon on the theme of "one more river to cross." The congregation in St. Columba Church listened with rapt attention as he said, "We crossed the Nile. We crossed the Mississippi. We crossed the mighty Ohio. But the river we've got to cross downtown today isn't a physical river. It's a river of the spirit." Urging his listeners to go out on the picket lines, he said, "We're going to picket downtown as long as there is a downtown." Later that day, Lukas witnessed violence and heard gunshots that continued until police cleared the streets.[23]

In 2007, another writer for the *New York Times* came to Cairo on a spring day and watched city workers cut weeds that were sprouting from the empty sidewalks around an empty theater and empty shops. In the red brick public library, he met Preston Ewing, then seventy-three years old, a tall, lanky, gray-haired man. Ewing told him that many white people blamed the boycotts and demonstrations for the city's decline, but he did not believe the explanation was that simple. He and other citizens were trying to preserve historic buildings like the library and the Custom House, and he still had hope that Cairo could have a renaissance. The reporter watched him press promotional brochures into visitors' hands.[24]

It would be pointless now to assert that Cairo should have prospered because of its location at the convergence of two great rivers. From the very beginning, the city struggled with natural and man-made disasters. Racism, segregation, and the civil rights battles of the 1960s and 1970s added a terrible chapter to the city's sad history, but Cairo's troubles began long before 1960. In the nineteenth and twentieth centuries, the local economy advanced in fits and starts. Destructive floods disrupted commerce, and drainage problems threatened people's health. There is no single cause of the city's long succession of troubles, but some of its woes came straight from the river.

CHAPTER TEN

Engineers

The engineer and the engineers' room on the *Admiral*
From the Collections of the St. Louis Mercantile Library at the University of Missouri–St. Louis

"When I give the engineer the Jingle, why, he knows I mean for him to give her all she's got."

—Mr. Pepper, the pilot, in Edna Ferber's *Show Boat*

It was the engineers' job to keep the boats moving and keep the people on them safe. In the early days of steamboating, engineers typically learned their skills on the job, spent their time in hot and greasy engine rooms, and responded to the pilots' jingling bells. As the steamboat era gave way to the modern era of barges and towboats, teams of professionally trained engineers systematically improved the river by installing a system of lights and markers, altering banks and building levees, and dredging to deepen channels and make the river more navigable. Engineers also engaged in flood-control efforts that protected life and property in the Mississippi valley.

Old-time river engineers had to be good blacksmiths. Generally, each boat carried a forge. Before a run, the engineer and his helpers inspected and repaired the machinery. They also made and mended chains for hoisting, hauling, and securing heavy objects. As mentioned previously, Louis Cavalier served as a blacksmith on the *Mandan*, but in fact he probably worked as an engineer. He received about the same pay as the pilot Charles Ellison. Court records from 1822 indicate that the boat's owners paid $25.00 to Ellison and $28.00 to Cavalier.[1]

In the nineteenth century, steamboat engineers did very hard and dangerous work, and many of them did it with insufficient training. Most began as "cubs," who oiled and cleaned the machinery and attended the boilers. Gradually, a cub learned to repair and operate the machinery and worked his way up to the position of engineer. Many engineers, at least in the early years of steamboating, had very limited knowledge of how the equipment worked. Responding to signals from the pilot, the engineer had to start, stop, and change speed many times a day in all kinds of weather and in many difficult bends of the river. The roiling currents of the river, snaggings, groundings, and other accidents caused leaking joints, cracked pipes, and other dangerous weaknesses that too often led to breakdowns and explosions.[2]

After the Civil War, the U.S. Army Corps of Engineers (Corps) increasingly applied scientific principles to river navigation. Engineering crews in survey boats explored, studied, and mapped every bank, channel, island, and sandbar on the Mississippi. Snag boats systematically removed tree limbs and other obstacles from the river. The Corps developed dredge boats that could scrape the sand from the river bottom and deepen the channels. As steamboats gave way to towboats and barges, the Corps built dikes and hurdles to protect the banks and regularize the river channel. By 1900, the Corps had made great progress in improving the harbors and facilitating river travel between St. Louis and Memphis, although ice and floods constantly plagued boat operators and the residents of river towns.[3]

As population in the Mississippi valley increased, the Corps became more deeply involved in flood control. After the 1927 flood, the Corps developed public works that had a dramatic impact on the stretch of river between Cairo and New Madrid. To prevent a repeat of the calamity, Major General Edgar Jadwin, chief of the Corps, proposed a new system of levees and floodways. According to Jadwin, a very serious flooding problem began at Cairo on the east bank of the river just north of Bird's Point, Missouri, on the west bank. In Jadwin's words, "From here to New Madrid the main levee on the west bank chokes the river unduly and should be set back sufficiently to lower the head of the water at Cairo by six [feet] in an extreme flood." The plan he proposed would save Cairo by creating a floodway, routing the overflow to a huge tract of Missouri farmland.[4]

Completed in 1933, the Bird's Point–New Madrid Floodway encompassed 131,000 acres of Missouri farmland from Bird's Point in northern Mississippi County to the city of New Madrid in New Madrid County, thirty-five miles to the south. To create this floodway, the Corps lowered the main levee and constructed a setback levee farther away from the river. In the event of another great flood, the Corps retained the right to deliberately breach the main levee near Bird's Point, allowing the water to flow through the floodway and reenter the Mississippi River just north of New Madrid. The Corps viewed the Bird's Point–New Madrid Floodway as a small part of a comprehensive flood-control system in the Mississippi valley.[5]

In January 1937 another massive flood of the Ohio and Mississippi rivers caused damage and suffering in twelve states. Rapidly rising water, in the bitter cold of winter, affected people from Pennsylvania to Louisiana. Nearly a million people were forced from their homes. In Louisville, Kentucky, more than half the city's population vacated flooded neighborhoods. In Cincinnati, Ohio, oil tanks collapsed, causing dozens of fires. In Paducah, Kentucky, officials ordered 35,000 people to evacuate. On January 16, levees broke along the St. Francis River in southeastern Missouri. By the end of the month, record flood levels on the Mississippi River threatened to inundate the 14,000 residents of Cairo. To combat this "super flood," the army used two thousand pounds of dynamite to blow the main levee.[6]

People in southeastern Missouri were not prepared for the sudden inundation after the Corps breached the levee. On the afternoon of January 26, residents up to fifty miles from the levee heard and felt a series of "tremendous blasts" and felt tremors. About three thousand people fled the floodway. Most residents had gotten out in the two days before the event, but some failed to receive the Corps' warning and had to flee from the surging waters that filled the setback basin. In a telegram dated January 27, 1937, the day after the breach, Major Roy D. Burdick of the Corps of Engineers asked Lieutenant Colonel P. S. Reinecke, the District Engineer in St. Louis, to send clothing and equipment for 2,500 refugees in Charleston, Missouri. The highway department had to send rescuers in motorboats. Many people walked or tried to escape in wagons with floodwater sloshing up around their feet and thick, roiling mud dragging at the wagon wheels. Others went back into the basin, risking their lives, to try and salvage livestock and personal possessions. Throughout the last week of January and the first weeks of February, people emerged out of the flooded river bottoms. On January 28, the *Scott County Democrat* reported that five hundred families sought refuge in New Madrid.[7]

The damages to life and property were appalling. In response to the chaos, the army hastily recruited men to shore up the setback levee. Several days after the levee breach, a barge crammed with more than a hundred workers sank in the roiling ice water. More than twenty men drowned in the disaster, which the coroner's jury blamed on negligence due to confused and hurried preparation for dealing with the flood. Damages in the Bird's Point–New Madrid floodway far exceeded a million dollars. A federal government report issued in March 1937 indicated that 1,500 farmers suffered property damage when more than 130,000 acres of land overflowed. Floodwaters destroyed five hundred buildings and killed half the livestock in the basin. At the time of the flood there were six villages in the basin: Bayouville, Belmont, Crosno, Dorena, Medley, and Wolf Island. Only two—Dorena and Wolf Island—survived. The people in the other four communities lost not only their livestock but also their crops and their homes.[8]

Two years after the flood, the hard-pressed sharecroppers of southeastern Missouri camped out on the roadsides in a dramatic plea for social justice. Owen Whitfield, an African American preacher and sharecropper, learned from his experience in the 1937 flood that the farm workers' condition was man-made and could be alleviated by human action. By the mid-1930s, the Southern Tenant Farmer' Union (STFU) began recruiting workers in the Missouri Bootheel. Thad Snow, a defiant cotton planter, invited the STFU to organize the workers on his farm in

Mississippi County. Whitfield joined the union in 1937, the year of the flood. Although he did not work on Snow's farm, he and Snow struck up an unusual friendship. Snow called Whitfield "the smartest organizer in Missouri," and two years later in 1939, the preacher used his eloquence and charisma to lead black and white sharecroppers and tenant farmers, displaced by the Depression, in a massive demonstration along Highways 60 and 61 in southeastern Missouri. As a result of the sharecroppers' peaceful action, the federal government began providing housing and other assistance for displaced farmworkers in southeastern Missouri.[9]

The Corps' efforts to tame the powerful river continued throughout the twentieth century. In addition to flood-control actions, the army operated fleets of survey boats, snag boats, and dredge boats. On the survey boats, crews of civilians sounded, measured, marked, and mapped the river to make it safe for towboats and barges. One of their jobs was setting out buoys to warn pilots about sandbars and other obstacles and guide them to open channels. As the vessels moved back and forth, leadsmen sounded the depths, and deckhands dropped red-and-black buoys into the roiling water. When the river shifted, the crews removed old buoys by lassoing them with ropes. On every trip up and down the river, survey crews collected data for use in drawing and revising detailed maps.[10]

Crews on the snag boats prowled the river in all kinds of weather, searching for submerged logs, snapped limbs, and debris from storms. These boats had u-shaped prows with huge metal tongs. The tongs could grab a giant tree and lift it out of the water. Deckhands would then use giant saws to chop the lumber into small sections that could safely float downstream. Their work was dangerous and never-ending. They might just have cleared a particular stretch of river and then see a storm wreak havoc and force them to do it all over again. Once in a while, they would bring up a hollow log full of big Mississippi catfish. They tended to be rough and adventurous men. The government allowed no gambling or drinking on the boats, but there were plenty of bars and poker games in towns along the riverbanks.[11]

Dredge boats were mammoth vessels with large crews of about fifty-six men, divided into three shifts. One shift would be off while two were on duty, alternately running the dredge. The hierarchy was similar to that on the steamboats and towboats. Officers would include the captain, the pilot, the first mate, and the chief engineer. The captain, the pilot, and the first mate all had master's (captain's) licenses, so that any one of them could cover for one of the others on their days off. In addition to the first mate, there would be a mate for each watch. Other crew members included engineers and firemen, head deckhands, regular deckhands, cooks, dishwashers, and "sailor men" (who changed bunks and did general clean-up).[12]

Don Bader of Ste. Genevieve began working for the Corps in 1952 and retired in 1984. He started his career as a deckhand and worked his way up to the position of second mate, first mate, assistant pilot, permanent pilot, and then captain of the *Kennedy*. The *Kennedy* was a gigantic "dust-pan" that moved upstream extending long mechanical arms that scooped sand and silt from the river bottom. Conditions could be pretty miserable in winter, when ice collected on the complicated system of cables and pipes, and in summer, when the crew had to work in hot, humid conditions. But it was satisfying work, he said in an interview, especially in the 1960s and 1970s when he had a good crew of men who were really devoted to the job.[13]

Carl Okenfuss of Ste. Genevieve was a third-generation riverman for the Corps. "My grandfather and father both retired from the Army Engineers," he said in an interview. "They worked on the dredge boats, and I guess between us we've got well over one hundred years of service." Carl served in the U.S. Navy for four years, beginning in 1969, and when he came home, he got a job on the river. "Being from Ste. Genevieve, some of the better jobs were on the river, and like I said, there were connections. Where I went to work, that's where my grandfather and father worked. Everybody knew them, and it was easy to get a deck hand's job." He worked as a deckhand for about eight years.[14]

Eventually, Okenfuss earned a master's license from the Coast Guard, allowing him to operate a vessel. All pilots and captains had to obtain this license. In the early 1980s, he went to work for Claude N. Strauser in the survey division of the Corps. Under Strauser's supervision, Okenfuss served as captain of three different motor vessels (the *Moore*, the *Simpson*, and the *Blankenship*), surveying and mapping the river's bottom and contours. The survey boats would go out and locate trouble spots. When they found a problem, they would call the dredge boat.[15]

Okenfuss worked for the Corps for thirty-seven years. For most of that time, he traveled from Hannibal to Cairo on the Mississippi River within the Corps' St. Louis District. "We also had thirty-six miles of the Kaskaskia River that's navigable, the lower eighty miles of the Illinois River, and

The modern towboat *Mississippi* at an upgraded landing From the Collection of the Cape River Heritage Museum, Cape Girardeau

occasionally when another district needed help with dredging, we'd send the dredge boats there. We went up the Ohio River, the Missouri River, and up to the Upper River, even above Hannibal, and down to the lower river. From Cairo south is what they call the lower river. And we went down there too depending on what they needed." Generally, his schedule was eight days on and four days off or seven days on and three days off. "And you could do that basically running in the St. Louis District. It wasn't too far on your days off to go home."[16]

His most difficult time on the job was during the 1993 flood. "You had three rivers crest at their all-time highs at the same time. Right above St. Louis, the Missouri, the Illinois, and the Mississippi, all at the same time. Boom. Boom. Boom." In Ste. Genevieve, he remembered, "They had half a dozen levee breaks." He was operating a survey boat. "We'd leave out of St. Louis, and we'd make our way through the trees to the levee, inside the levee. When a levee breaks, it usually eats out a tremendous amount of area behind it when the water starts in." At that time, the Corps had just started using Global Positioning Systems (GPS). Okenfuss and his crew were able to install GPS monitoring devices inside the levee where there were openings. "And so," he recalled, "the river hadn't even crested yet, and we already had a picture of what they would need to repair the breach. They [the Corps] could let the contracts before the water level went down—to repair it."[17]

Looking back on his career, Okenfuss had one regret. If he had the chance to do it again, he said he would go to college. "But I made my family a good living, and retirement is good." What he loved most about the river were the spots "where you can get out and there's nothing for miles. Like Tower Rock."[18]

Don Bader also loved working on the river. The one thing he hated was leaving his family for days at a time. "But once I got on the boat," he said, "I loved my damn job. I really did." He loved the satisfaction of getting the work done, and he loved being out there on the water. "It's never the same. When you get up in the morning and look out at the river, it's never the same as it was the night before. You're moving, although it may only be twenty-five feet every ten minutes. You look out the window and it's never the same."[19]

The ever-changing river
From the Collection of the Cape River Heritage Museum, Cape Girardeau

CHAPTER ELEVEN

New Madrid, Missouri

The New Madrid steamboat landing
An illustration from *Harper's Weekly*, March 10, 1883.
From the Collections of the St. Louis Mercantile Library
at the University of Missouri–St. Louis

> **The town of New Madrid was looking very unwell [due to a flood in 1882]; but otherwise unchanged from its former condition and aspect. Its blocks of frame houses were still grouped in the same old flat plain, and environed by the same old forests.**
>
> Mark Twain, *Life on the Mississippi*

New Madrid originated in the 1780s as a trading post known as "Lagraisse" or "L'Anse a la Graisse" (cove of fat grease), so named because of the bear meat stored there. From this location on a bend in the Mississippi River, French traders did business with Native American tribes and transported furs upriver to Kaskaskia. In 1787, a Philadelphia trader and Revolutionary War veteran, Colonel George Morgan, received a Spanish land grant encompassing Lagraisse and began making plans for a grand city that would serve as a port of entry between the United States and Spanish territory. For this city he proposed the name "Nuevo Madrid," New Madrid.[1]

Morgan's grandiose dream did not quite materialize, but by the 1790s New Madrid had become a hub of Native American, French, and Anglo American settlement and a center of governmental activity. In the years before the Louisiana Purchase, boats going up- and downriver had to stop at New Madrid for inspection by Spanish officials. When the Spanish government relinquished jurisdiction, the United States sent soldiers to protect the river port, as relationships with the Native American tribes began to deteriorate. In the early nineteenth century, New Madrid continued to prosper as an important stopping place on the river, a center for trade in furs and grain, and a point of inspection for vessels traveling from or to New Orleans.[2]

New Madrid's name is forever linked with a series of earthquakes in late 1811 and early 1812 that dramatically changed the course of the river. The shocks began in mid-December and continued into the following February. During this time period, William Leigh Pierce was traveling with a convoy of flatboats carrying goods down the Mississippi. At two o'clock on the morning of December 16, he and his fellow boatmen, moored a little way below New Madrid, felt a sudden, violent movement of their boats and heard a terrible clattering of tree branches. There were several shocks in quick succession, as the trees around them shook, and a large oak tree snapped in two. At dawn, just after the crews untied their boats, another shock loosened the riverbank, and trees crashed into the water. Pierce sent accounts of his experience to several publications.[3]

In and around New Madrid, people began to leave their houses for fear of chimneys and other structures collapsing. By February 7, observers had reported that all the houses in town had caved in completely or lost their roofs and chimneys. On that day, the last remaining inhabitants fled the town, escaping to the nearest places of refuge from a blasted landscape of fallen trees, flooded streams, cracked and broken fields, and eruptions of sand. Throughout the period of the quakes, portions of the river bank collapsed, and the river flowed into new channels. When people returned to take a look at the site of their town, the ground had sunk beneath it. In the spring the river swallowed it up.[4]

Gradually, in the years after the earthquake, residents rebuilt the town on what seemed safe locations, but the river kept encroaching, and the community's growth was slow. Strong tremors continued through the spring of 1812, and with decreasing intensity, for nearly a decade after that. Before the quakes, there had been about a hundred houses in New Madrid. Only twenty houses were there in 1817. Population began to grow in the 1830s and 1840s, but the town still suffered from periodic floods that washed away the riverfront. In 1846, Sir Charles Lyell, a British geologist, visited New Madrid and found it rather dreary. There was no hotel, so he and his wife had to stay in a spare room belonging to a baker. On the riverbank Lyell saw several recently fallen houses and predicted that within a few years steamboats would pass over the site of the house where he and his wife had found lodging. He was correct.[5]

One early settler who stayed in New Madrid and prospered after the earthquake was Robert Goah Watson, a Scottish-born trader. His daughter Amanda Jane became a prominent local figure. In 1836, at the age of eighteen, Amanda married William Washington Hunter and subsequently gave birth to seven children. She also helped with the family farm and business enterprises, including a mercantile establishment called the Crystal Palace and a steamboat that carried textiles. When her husband died of yellow fever in 1859, Amanda went on supervising the construction of an elegant home. It was completed around 1860, and when the Civil War began, her property included not only that house but large landholdings and more than thirty slaves. After the war, the family continued to live on the property, and some of their former slaves remained in their employ.[6]

The Hunter family almost surely vacated their home in March 1862 as Union and Confederate forces converged on New Madrid. Finding the streets nearly empty, Confederate soldiers looted houses and stores and gutted the courthouse, as a Confederate flotilla gathered along the riverbank. By a strange coincidence, one of the men on the Confederate ship *McRae* was James Morris Morgan, great-grandson of George Morgan. As Union forces came closer to the town, Flag-Officer George Hollins ordered Morgan to go ashore and set fire to a line of houses. Morgan wrote in his memoirs that he went to a barn filled with hay and lit a match. The wind quickly fanned the flames, as Morgan and his men ran back to the vessel.[7]

On March 12, at dawn, Union soldiers led by General John Pope began a heavy bombardment of the Confederate fortifications in New Madrid. Confederate general John P. McCown, with a much smaller force, returned fire all day long and into the next day. During the night of March 13, the Confederates fled under cover of a heavy thunderstorm. When Pope entered town the next day, he found discarded clothing, unfinished meals, empty tents, and abandoned horses, mules, and ammunition. By noon on March 15, naval commander Andrew H. Foote and a flotilla of gunboats had closed in on Island Number 10 and begun a siege that would last until April 8, when the Confederates' defenses collapsed.[8]

The prize gained by the Union, Island Number 10, gradually sank into insignificance. In *Life on the Mississippi,* Twain wrote that the river had changed greatly. The island he remembered from his earlier life as a pilot was three miles long and a quarter of a mile wide, but by the 1880s "one had to hunt for it with a spy glass." In wartime, it had been an important place, commanding a view of a long stretch of river, and heavily fortified. Two decades later, powerful currents had reduced the island, a place that caused terrible suffering, to "an insignificant little tuft." [9]

Twain also observed the pall cast over New Madrid by the 1882 flood. In March of that year, water rushed into the town and covered streets, yards, and gardens. Skiffs, rafts, canoes, and planks carried people up and down the main street. Refugees from the submerged countryside crowded into those houses that stood on high ground. Difficult tasks were made harder. For instance, when a four-year-old girl died, friends and relatives had to travel in boats to the funeral. A man who lived on Wolf Island just upriver from New Madrid lost six children when his boat capsized as he tried to rescue his family from the flood. The federal government sent the steamer *Anita* with supplies for all the families hit by the calamity, which Twain said would be remembered "for several generations."[10]

Persistent floods and heavily wooded swamps slowed development of the rich farmland around New Madrid in Missouri's southeastern Bootheel. Regional boosters had long pleaded with the state government to support swamp drainage. In 1851, Representative Robert A. Hatcher of New Madrid County pushed a bill through the legislature, creating a special reclamation district in the counties of southeastern Missouri containing swamps or overflowed lands. Within two years, however, the state turned responsibility for drainage back to individual counties. Settlers and developers bypassed the region, and industrialization and urbanization proceeded all around it.[11]

In the late nineteenth century, Louis Houck zealously promoted development in the area. Convinced of the Bootheel's economic potential, Houck oversaw construction of a network of short-line railroads connecting the swampy lowlands to timber markets in Cape Girardeau, St. Louis, and other urban centers. He carried on a lively correspondence with lumber tycoons, persuading them to move to the area. Lumber companies built sawmills and planing mills along Houck's railroad lines and bought huge tracts of forest. Within a few decades these companies transformed the Bootheel from forested wetland to a long, flat stretch of fertile fields. Local newspapers dubbed Houck the "Father of Southeast Missouri."[12]

By 1905, regional boosters had opened the way for drainage of the Bootheel swamps. In January of that year, supporters of economic development formed the Little River Drainage District, a public agency that planned and constructed an enormous system of ditches, canals, and levees to carry water from the overflowed lands and channel it into the Mississippi River. District boundaries stretched from Cape Girardeau to the Missouri-Arkansas line, encompassing an area of 540,000 acres that included New Madrid County and six other counties. This massive drainage effort completed the task of opening the rich land to agriculture.[13]

Between 1900 and 1930, the population of the Bootheel region skyrocketed, and social tensions increased as cotton cultivation took hold and flourished. As planters, ginners, and entrepreneurs discovered the area's potential, the population of New Madrid County soared from 7,694 in 1880 to 30,262 in 1930. Sharecroppers and tenant farmers migrated from Arkansas and other southern states, increasing the African American population dramatically. In New Madrid County, the black population increased from 2,027 in 1900 to 5,617 in 1930. Rapid growth and an economic system that created sharp divisions between prosperous landowners and impoverished tenants brought about social instability and escalating racial conflict in the early decades of the twentieth century.[14]

The sharecroppers' situation became desperate during the Great Depression of the 1930s, and the federal government tried to address the problem of farm tenancy. Under the auspices of the Federal Emergency Relief Administration (FERA), the Farm Security Administration (FSA) created an experimental community on a tract of farmland north of New Madrid near the village of La Forge. Planning for the project began in the flood year of 1937, but construction of housing did not begin in earnest until 1938. Lonnie Stover, his wife, three children, and blind father, moved from a leaky two-room shack into the first weatherproof four-room dwelling at La Forge during that rainy spring. The four- and five-room houses in the project had living rooms, kitchen/dining areas, two or three bedrooms, and screened-in porches. Each house also had a barn, a well, and a sanitary outhouse, and each family received a cow, a sow, two shoats, fifty chickens and one team of mules. The goal of the project was to give sharecroppers a chance to become self-sufficient farmers and householders.[15]

One of the residents at La Forge was Owen Whitfield, who led the Sharecroppers' Roadside Demonstration in 1939. Although he and his family had found a haven in the experimental community, Whitfield could not forget that thousands of other farm workers were homeless. After organizing the demonstration, he went to St. Louis to solicit support from churches, labor organizations, and other sympathetic groups. While he was gone, local authorities searched for him at La Forge. For a short time, suspicion fell on Hans Baasch, the manager of the housing project, as the probable mastermind of the demonstration, but soon people's animosity focused on Whitfield's friend Thad Snow. In the aftermath of the demonstration, the federal government established additional housing projects in the Bootheel, and gradually tensions died down.[16]

The dramatic events of the 1930s caused Snow and others to think critically about the changes that had been brought to the Bootheel by the railroads, logging, swamp drainage, flood control, and in particular the Bird's Point–New Madrid Floodway. In 1937, several months after the January flood, Snow's friend L. T. Berthe came to him with a rambling manuscript, full of facts and figures, criticizing the Corps for what he considered its botched attempt to control the behavior of the Mississippi River. Berthe wanted to publish the tract but lacked funds. Snow edited the piece and added some of his own firsthand observations of the effects of the levee breach on the people in the floodway. Together Berthe and Snow arranged to have the booklet printed under the title "Old Man River Speaks" on slick paper with illustrations, maps, and graphs.[17]

Snow and Berthe continued to call attention to problems with the floodway throughout the 1930s and 1940s. By 1949, county courts, city administrators, and citizens of Mississippi and New Madrid counties had become very disgruntled and appealed to Congress for a solution to drainage problems exacerbated by the post-1927 flood-control program. Construction of the setback levee had effectively dammed many drainage ditches, leaving much of the farmland west of the levee without an outlet for excess water. The Corps' diversion channel, which was supposed to provide that outlet, did not function properly because in some places it was as much as eight feet higher than the drainage ditches. When Berthe fell ill, Snow took the lead and kept up the pressure on the Corps, reporting that sandbags were often required to protect the state road along the lake bank near his property, but he began to wonder if there would ever be a satisfactory solution to what he called the "drainage dilemma." Before he passed way in 1955, he deeply regretted the changes that deforestation and swamp drainage had brought to the Bootheel.[18]

Over the years, many other people embraced the cause of saving the remnants of the original landscape of southeastern Missouri. In the late 1930s, in spite of the Depression, local citizens, including schoolchildren, contributed and collected money to purchase the region's last tract of virgin hardwoods and save them from loggers. The tall trees on this piece of land stood out like sentinels above the great stretch of water in the floodway after the levee breach in 1937. The following year, the State of Missouri acquired the eighty-acre tract and an additional 920 acres of land around it to establish Big Oak Tree State Park in Mississippi County. In 1986, the original tract of virgin forest was recognized as a National Natural Landmark.[19]

In 1967, the state of Missouri committed to preserving the site of a fortified Indian village on a sandy eminence called Pinhook Ridge inside the floodway. Archaeological investigations, conducted by the state in cooperation with the University of Missouri, uncovered evidence of three or four stockades on the top of a large man-made mound on the site known as Towosahgy (Old Town). Subsequent investigations revealed that the site was occupied from about AD 400 to 1420 by Mississippian people, who fished, hunted, and farmed in the river valley. Missouri's Department of Natural Resources, recognizing the importance of these discoveries, created and maintained the area as Towosahgy State Historic Site.[20]

For seventy-five years, from 1937 until the catastrophic flood of 2011, despite several floods, Missouri politicians successfully fought against the breaching of the Bird's Point levee. The Corps refrained from taking this action even during the great flood of 1993. During these decades, the Corps allowed development within the floodway, and farmers continuously cultivated the land. The population of Cairo decreased during this period, and the floodway population never regained 1937 levels. When catastrophic flood levels came again in 2011, Cairo's population was three thousand, and there were two hundred residents occupying ninety homes in the floodway.[21]

In early May 2011, Major General Michael J. Walsh authorized a series of explosions that blew out more than 11,000 feet of the levee, releasing a gigantic surge of water into the floodway. His intention was to save Cairo from imminent destruction. On Monday, May 2, the river reached a record depth of 61.7 feet at Cairo, nearly topping the 62-foot levee. By Tuesday afternoon, the crest had fallen to 60.1 feet, saving the town. But the water that was released into the floodway rose nearly to the tops of the trees at Big Oak Tree State Park, covered all but the summit of the big mound at Towosahgy, tore through houses and barns, covered farmers' fields, and devastated two communities.[22]

Residents of Morehouse and Pinhook surveyed their losses in the summer after the levee breach. By August 2011, more than sixty damaged houses in Morehouse had been razed, but residents still expressed a desire to rebuild their town. In Pinhook, the flood left a cluster of homes with sagging wooden floors, wrecked porches, and broken windows. During the flood, the village's thirty residents, who were mostly African Americans, had gone to the nearby towns of East Prairie and Sikeston or to more distant places, where friends and relatives gave them shelter. In meetings with government officials, most of Pinhook's residents said they felt an emotional attachment to their community, but they had no intention of going back.[23]

The flood of 2011 was bigger than those of 1927 and 1937, and, according to officials, the flood-control system worked. George Grugett, executive vice president of the Mississippi Valley Flood Control Association, explained that the massive overflow passed through the Mississippi valley without any loss of life. As Grugett wrote in a newspaper editorial, "There was not a single unintended overtopping or crevassing of the mainline levee and not one acre was flooded that was not designed to be flooded." This is small comfort to the people of Pinhook or the residents of the flooded town of Morehouse or the floodway farmers: they took no solace from the knowledge that their losses were intended and "designed."[24]

The history of New Madrid and southeastern Missouri is filled with disasters—both natural and man-made. The earthquake of 1812 gave the town and its environs a bad reputation that kept many settlers away. A series of floods in the nineteenth and twentieth centuries slowed economic development. Swamp drainage and flood-control projects brought the lumber industry to the area and opened up rich land for farming, but progress came at great cost. The region's troubled history and stubborn survival bear witness to human endurance but challenge the idea that the natural world, and especially the Mississippi River, are subject to "design" or control. Despite the best efforts of governments and planners, in all of life there is an element of chance.

CHAPTER TWELVE

Confidence Men and Gamblers

Passengers in a floating palace
From the Collection of the Cape River Heritage
Museum, Cape Girardeau

He had come aboard the *Lady Lee* at St. Louis, his finances low, his hopes high, his erstwhile elegant garments in their present precarious state. He had planned, following the game of stud poker in which he immediately immersed himself, to come ashore at Memphis or, at the latest Natchez, with his finances raised to the high level of his hopes.

—Edna Ferber, *Show Boat*

In Herman Melville's novel *The Confidence Man* (first published in 1857), a crowd of strangers boards a riverboat in St. Louis and embarks on a trip downriver. On the decks, promenades, and balconies of the great floating palace, a wide variety of individuals, including "Northern speculators and Eastern philosophers, English, Irish, German, Scotch, Danes; Santa Fe traders in striped blankets," men and women of all types, mingle and clash in brief episodes that end at the next nondescript landing. At every town along the way, some passengers vanish, and new ones appear. Among them are furtive, seemingly ghostly figures who may or may not be what they seem: a deaf-mute displaying biblical placards, a crippled mendicant, an importunate mourner, a man soliciting funds for charity, a man selling stock in a coal company, an herb-doctor. All of these people are trying, in one way or another, to steal money from gullible victims.[1]

Melville's confidence man takes a more urbane form at a later point in the novel, when the boat is docked at Cairo on a damp summer evening "fanned with mosquitoes, and sparkling with fireflies." A stranger arrives, slaps a fellow passenger on the back, and strikes up a conversation. The passenger, who has already encountered several shady characters on the voyage, demands to know who the newcomer really is. "A cosmopolitan," says the conman, "a catholic man, who being such, ties himself to no narrow tailor or teacher, but federates, in heart as in costume, something of the various gallantries of men under various suns." In other words, he is no one; or he could be anyone. "You are another one of them," says the target of his evil intentions. "Out of my sight!"[2]

In Melville's time Americans were gaining an awareness of professional thieves and tricksters. Rapid social change, industrialization, and urbanization in the mid-nineteenth century unleashed a growing number of unsupervised young men, who could easily be victimized by cunning strangers. Ambitious young men could just as easily become shrewd and ruthless predators themselves. In the mid-1840s a New Yorker named Jonathan Green abandoned the gaming tables and began to write books exposing the evil ways of professional gamblers. New York newspapermen first used the term "confidence man" in 1849 while covering the arrest of William Thompson, who tricked a number of gentlemen out of their gold watches. Melville, a New Yorker, almost certainly was aware of Green's anti-gambling crusade and Thompson's infamous behavior. New York was a city full of strangers. In Melville's novel, a Mississippi riverboat became a surrogate for the city, a place where people could come and go quickly and anonymously, appearing and reappearing in many different guises, concealing their true natures and dark purposes.[3]

"River sharpers," or professional card players, traveled on the riverboats, taking advantage of Americans' love for games of chance. Gambling was common in the Mississippi valley even before steamboats came chugging up and down the river. Passing through Ste. Genevieve in 1808, a traveler named Christian Schultz noted that card games were popular with both the French and the Anglo American settlers. At balls given by the most religious and traditional of the residents, there was always a room set aside for gambling. Somewhat amazed, Schultz remarked, "Never did I see people with so much spirit and perseverance to win each other's money, as in this little village." Players would sit for many hours at the card table with no food, only coffee and wine. The stakes could be high, even hundred of dollars, but the players were people who knew one another, who likely met on a daily basis. When steamboats began plying the river, strangers would gather around card tables where the games never seemed to stop, but the players could vanish at the next landing.[4]

The vast majority of the male passengers participated in gambling, although most of the women abstained. If the men did not play the games themselves, they watched or placed side bets on the players. Most of them, of course, were not professionals, just ordinary people, freed for a short time from the normal restraints of proper behavior. But some men traveled on the steamboats for the sole purpose of gambling. These men did not stay on any particular boat for very long, and they could quickly disappear into the crowds, the darkness, or the woods at any landing. They did not play for sport, and they intended to win by any means necessary. This was the way they made their living.[5]

Some captains took a hard line against these games, but others tolerated them. It seems likely that some captains were not above accepting a cut of the winnings in exchange for their tolerance. Other members of the crew also profited from the gamblers' activities. In many cases, the gamblers paid well for the best sleeping quarters and lavishly tipped the cabin boys. Bartenders also stood to gain from generous tips. Big money changed hands, although historian Louis Hunter maintains that many commonly accepted tales have exaggerated the amounts won and lost. Steamboat companies generally turned a blind eye to these practices, because professional gamblers made up a sizable percentage of total passengers.[6]

John Morris, a self-styled vagabond, wrote about his experiences on the "turgid and treacherous" waters of the Mississippi in the 1830s. Onboard the steamboat *Mediator* he remembered that there were five or six lively card tables every night. Passengers, who had nothing better to do, gathered around and watched the players. Card sharpers, who traveled in small groups, pretended to be total strangers to each other. Some of them played at the tables; others mingled with the crowd. These men were experts at cheating. The ones who took part in the games used bottom-dealing, false cutting, tricky shuffling, and card-palming to manipulate the game. The ones who stood and watched passed information to the crooked players about the other players' cards.[7]

Like other confidence men, riverboat gamblers used role-playing and disguises to lure gullible strangers with money in their pockets and time on their hands into games they were sure to lose. Riverboat gamblers tended to work together in teams of four to six men, with team members playing various parts. While one posed as a slow-talking cowboy, another might appear to be a shrewd, fast-talking salesman. In these roles, they would encourage other passengers to get into the game and bet more money. Some professional gamblers dressed to give the impression that they were from the southern planter class. Others found it more profitable to behave as though they were ignorant backwoodsmen who had never seen a gaming table. One might change his appearance in the middle of a trip. If an enraged passenger complained to the captain, a gambler might have to hastily exit the scene, either by getting off the boat or by changing his appearance.[8]

Don Kimball, one of the most successful gamblers on the Mississippi River, recalled that every now and then a "mark" would cause an uproar, and the captain would round up the professional gamblers and kick them off the boat. In these situations, he said, "The boys used to have false whiskers and wigs" so that the aggrieved party would not recognize them. If there was no time to put on a disguise, they might have to take desperate measures. "Many a time," said Kimball, "I've known them to jump off the boat into the water before the boat landed, to get away before the kick was made and the victim could look at the passengers to find out his man." During his career in the 1850s and 1860s, he swam ashore numerous times. Once he reached land, though, he had little to fear. Looking back on these years after his retirement in the 1890s, he said, "There wasn't much prosecuting if a fellow was caught."[9]

Some of the games were out and out swindles; others gave amateurs a fighting chance. Three-card monte was nothing but a shell game that used cards. Players bet on their ability to locate one of three cards that was first exposed and then placed face down. Shills made the game seem easy, but dealers used sleight-of-hand to make sure the player could never find the correct card. Faro was a popular and fast-paced game in which players bet that a particular card would turn up. The king of the betting games was poker, a slower-paced and more complex game, in which the stakes could rise dangerously high. Mirrors, marked cards, and "holdouts" (clips that helped a cheater stash cards under the table or up his sleeve) gave professional gamblers the edge but sometimes put their lives in jeopardy.[10]

In the heyday of steamboating, George Devol liked to deal three-card monte. In his own words, he "had a great graft" on the short stretch of the Missouri River between St. Louis and St. Charles. "We would go up on a boat and back by rail." On the boat on the way up, he and his partner, Posey Jeffers, took bets of from one dollar to ten thousand dollars that no one could pick out the winning card. One night a man pulled out a large roll of bills and put up five thousand dollars. Jeffers put up the same amount. The card that turned up was a loser, and the man bet the same amount a second time. After losing and paying up again, the man walked away "as if to lose $10,000 was an every-day thing with him."[11]

In the end, this incident demonstrated that the Mississippi valley was full of grifters. Devol and Jeffers closed up the game and patted themselves on the back. The next day, when they counted up their cash, they found that they had a stack of fresh new bills drawn on the State Bank of Missouri. But all ten thousand dollars' worth was counterfeit. Devol and his partner "deposited it in the (fire) bank, as we had no immediate use for it." The sucker had suckered them.[12]

Not everyone was in on the game, though, and fleecing innocent people could have sad consequences. In his memoirs, Devol recounted an incident on a boat near Memphis. His partner won $600 from a man at the poker table. When the man told his wife, she came out of their cabin with his pistol and yelled, "I will have that money back, or kill the man." Devol went to the bartender and asked for the unloaded gun he kept in a drawer. Devol looked at the woman and said he was on her side. "You would do right in shooting that fellow, for he is nothing but a gambler. I don't believe your pistol will go off; you had better take my pistol for

I am a government detective, and have to keep the best of arms." She exchanged her weapon.[13]

When Devol's partner came into firing range, the woman demanded her husband's money back. Passengers bolted from the area as she aimed the gun at the gambler's head. He stood firm, knowing she held an unloaded gun, explaining that he had won the money in a poker game and would not give it back. The woman fired, but the pistol did not go off. The gambler convinced her to go back to her cabin and calmed her down by giving her a hundred dollars. Devol took the bullets out of her pistol and returned it to her. While Devol's anecdotes were not always completely truthful, this story provides a believable glimpse of the human costs of the grifter's life.[14]

Devol and others have contributed to the romantic view of the riverboat gambler as a dashing and brave ne'er-do-well with a deep-seated sense of honor. In keeping with this image, Devol dressed like a wealthy southern planter in a long coat, high hat, gray trousers, ruffled shirt, silk tie, and diamond stickpin. His clothing marked him as a gentleman abiding by an aristocratic code of behavior. He liked to pass along stories of his courage in the face of physical threats, his cool acceptance of financial losses, his quick and ready wit, and his sense of justice. As the story goes, one of his victims was a minister who had just preached a sermon against gambling. Devol fleeced the man but then returned his money to him, admonishing him to "sin no more."[15]

Kimball had no illusions about the honesty of his trade but still remembered his fellow gamblers as admirable fellows. Of the practices of most professionals, he said, "That wasn't gambling—it was robbing." On the other hand, he recalled, "They were good fellows, free with their money as water after scheming to bust their heads to get it." They were heavy drinkers, as he told it, and they were clothes-conscious. Most of them dressed like gentlemen, but two men in particular stood out for their sartorial graces. "Gib Cohern and Tom Mackey were the dressers of the river," he said. "They'd send to Paris for their underclothing, and all that sort of thing." In many cases, they were profligate spenders. Kimball himself managed to hang on to only a few of the many thousands of dollars he won, but he kept enough to retire in California.[16]

The lives of gamblers often did not end so well. This was certainly true of John Powell, whom Kimball described as "the greatest all-round gambler that ever drew breath." Powell, a Missourian, owned a theater in New

Orleans, a farm in Tennessee, and property in St. Louis. Andrew Jackson and Stephen A. Douglas counted him as a friend. Kimball regarded him as an honest player, not a sharper, and one of the best poker players on the river. In 1858, at the age of fifty, he had achieved a level of success undreamed of by most gamblers, and people assumed that he would retire, but he kept playing, and his career ended in tragedy.[17]

On a trip downriver onboard the *Atlantic,* Powell got into a game with a handsome young Englishman who was planning to go to Texas. Kimball observed the game, which he said was "a square game," that lasted two days and two nights. Eventually, Powell won all of the young man's money. After turning over his bank checks and drafts one by one, the man went to his stateroom and brought up his luggage. He kept on playing until he had gambled away all his belongings, including his clothes, his watch, and his jewelry. Late in the evening, the game came to an end. The Englishman laughed, got up from the table, and went up on deck. Turning to Kimball, Powell remarked that he would give back the man's clothes and watch the next day.[18]

The next morning, Powell and Kimball were laughing and talking with several other men in the barroom. According to Kimball, the young man came in, smiling, and said he had paid dearly to learn American games. After that, he whirled around, drew a pistol, and shot himself through the heart. He staggered back into Powell's arms and died. Kimball and the other gamblers were stunned, and Powell seemed to go out of his mind. "He would sit up for days at a time," recalled Kimball, "doing nothing but smoke. He seemed to be in a daze, and we could not rouse him to anything." When he reached New Orleans, he had a banker send the money back to the young man's family.[19]

About a year later, he returned to the river, but he was inept and unlucky. Within another year, he had lost everything. During the Civil War, he hung around the gambling houses of New Orleans, and after that he went out west. The last time Kimball saw him he borrowed five dollars and said he had spent the last week sleeping in wagons on the streets of St. Louis. In 1870, he died, broke, in Virginia City, Nevada.[20]

By the end of the nineteenth century, riverboat gamblers had seen their last days. The big floating palaces filled with gullible passengers were vanishing from the river. Legendary figures like John Powell were passing sadly into history. Devol had written his memoirs, and Kimball, in retirement in California, was saying, nostalgically, "Those were great old times, and they'll never come back."[21]

Edna Ferber, a highly successful twentieth-century author, wrote a novel that firmly implanted a riverboat gambler named Gaylord Ravenal in twentieth-century American popular culture. The instant he made his appearance, "an idle elegant figure in garments whose modish cut and fine material served, at a distance to conceal their shabbiness," the heroine and the reader fell in love with him. With bloodshot eyes, frayed nerves, and tired face, after a poker game that lasted from St. Louis to New Orleans, he still had clean hands and "the habits and instincts of a gentleman." He was a stereotypical character, but a beguiling one, and he became even more memorable singing romantic ballads in the Broadway musical and the Hollywood film.[22]

A real riverboat gambler probably bore little resemblance to Ferber's romantic hero. He may have had more in common with the sly, elusive, and sinister confidence man of Melville's Mississippi River tale. He appeared in many forms, some more myth than fact, but for a time he played a vital and colorful part in the shadowy world of the river.

CHAPTER THIRTEEN

Memphis, Tennessee

The Memphis levee
From the Collections of the St. Louis Mercantile Library
at the University of Missouri–St. Louis

I rented a room in the Beale Street section and went to work. Outside, the lights flickered. Chitterling joints were as crowded as the more fashionable resorts like the Iroquois. Piano thumpers tickled the ivories in the saloons to attract customers, furnishing a theme for the prayers at Beale Street Baptist Church and Avery Chapel (Methodist). Scores of powerfully built roustabouts from river boats sauntered along the pavement.... All that contributed to the color and spell of Beale Street mingled outside, but I neither saw nor heard it that night. I had a song to write.

—W. C. Handy, *Father of the Blues*

In 1819, three speculators—Judge John Overton, General James Winchester, and General Andrew Jackson—founded Memphis on the bluffs overlooking the Mississippi in western Tennessee. At first, the site held only a trading post, a fort, and the cabins of a few settlers, but the town grew rapidly as a hub of river commerce. Outlying areas in the river bottoms developed as cotton plantations, and Memphis became a center for cotton marketing and the slave trade. In 1857, a major east-west railroad connected Memphis to Charleston, South Carolina. During the Civil War, the city also became the center of boat-building and war production for the Confederacy.[1]

Memphis fell to the Union after a naval battle on June 6, 1862. Crowds gathered on the levee, bluffs, and rooftops to watch as a Confederate fleet clashed with heavy Union ironclads. Thick smoke and roaring guns soon drove most of the spectators away, and when the smoke cleared, the Confederate boats were in shambles. After the battle, an influx of Union soldiers, followed by a desperate crew of prostitutes and gamblers, brought social tension and turbulence. Even more damaging was the disruption of commerce on the river, a terrible blow to the local economy.[2]

A shameful massacre took place at Fort Pillow, one of several forts on the Mississippi River north of Memphis and south of Island Number 10. In the spring of 1864, with Confederate hopes fading, General Nathan Bedford Forrest, a Memphis hero, decided to wrest Fort Pillow from Union control. On April 12, he led a brutal attack, wiping out an entire Union garrison. Half of the soldiers were white members of the Thirteenth Tennessee Union Cavalry, and half were black troops of the Sixth U.S. Colored Infantry. The vicious nature of the action reflected Forrest's racism, which he would continue to demonstrate after the war as a leader of the Ku Klux Klan.[3]

Another tragedy was in the making when war-weary passengers from the crowded decks of the steamboat *Sultana* spent a few precious hours on the Memphis levee on April 26, 1865. While roustabouts unloaded a heavy cargo of sugar, travelers made their way up the hill to shelters and saloons for hot meals and bracing drinks. Among them was a Union soldier named George Robinson, who had spent some time as a Confederate prisoner of war. Later that evening, military personnel rounded up the soldiers, as bells announced the steamboat's departure. Some of the passengers failed to make it back in time, but the auburn-haired Robinson bedded down on the promenade deck next to his friend John Corliss. At

2:00 am on April 27, the *Sultana*'s four boilers exploded, and the boat went down in a horrific blaze that killed 1,700 people, including Corliss. But Robinson survived.[4]

After the explosion, he woke up in the *Sultana*'s coal bin with his friend's lifeless body on his legs. He was in agony; his arms were scalded, and his breathing was labored. He had not heard the explosion, but he heard people moaning, and he also heard someone saying there was a way out. Climbing up out of the coal bin, he made his way to the deck, where men, women, children, horses, and mules were rushing out into the cold river. Robinson followed them into the water and climbed onto the floating body of a dead mule. On this strange flotation device, he drifted downriver to a point below Memphis, where rescuers pulled him out of the water and took him to Adams Hospital. Of the more than seven hundred people who initially survived the disaster, more than two hundred later died in Memphis hospitals. Robinson had chills, scalded arms, and injuries to his wrist and chest, but he lived.[5]

The river brought sorrow to Memphis in many different forms. At the foot of the bluffs, the shallow, muddy water in the bottomland provided a breeding ground for mosquitos that carried yellow fever. In 1867, this terrible disease took many lives, including those of iron molder George Jones and all four of his children. His widow, Mary, left the city and moved to Chicago, where she opened a dressmaking shop and began attending meetings of the Knights of Labor. When the great fire of 1871 destroyed her business, she became a labor organizer, known to most of the rank and file as Mother Jones. Her eloquence and her ability to understand the struggles of working men and their families eventually made her one of the most beloved figures in the United Mine Workers of America (UMWA) and one of the most famous women in the United States.[6]

When yellow fever again struck the city in the summer of 1873, its first victims were boatmen and their families in Happy Hollow, an ill-named, miserable collection of flatboats and shanties on stilts. Sufferers could be recognized by their yellow-tinged eyes and skin, and in the last stages of the illness, they vomited black bile. By the end of the season, hundreds of people in Memphis had died of this plague. In 1874, city officials demolished Happy Hollow, but the swamps and open sewers that bred the disease remained.[7]

During another outbreak of yellow fever in 1878, the first person to die was Kate Bionda, the Irish-born wife of man who owned a snack shop catering to boatmen. During that ghastly summer, city hospitals teemed with dying patients tended by doctors, nurses, priests, and nuns. With no effective treatments, doctors tried everything from hot baths to ice packs, castor oil, sage tea, and any patent medicine ever peddled to desperate people. Health officials doused streets and sidewalks with disinfectants and spread so much lime that it looked like drifted snow. Housekeepers burned piles of infected bedclothes. Hearses rolled constantly through the streets, and still the coffins piled up in front of houses and hotels. Before it was over, five thousand people would die, and thousands more would abandon the city.[8]

Seventeen heroic women, including sixteen nuns and one madam, died trying to save people during the epidemic. The madam, Annie Cook, became a local legend. She presided over the city's most lavish bordello. In August 1878, she discharged her fancy ladies and turned the Mansion House on Gayoso Street into a hospital. Lorena Meade, one of her ladies, stayed to help nurse the sick and dying. Cook had done this before in 1873, and when the news spread that she was doing it again, a group of women from Louisville, Kentucky, sent her a letter expressing their gratitude for the "noble example" she was setting for Christians. She died of yellow fever in September 1878.[9]

Cook, who was born in Ohio, had settled in Memphis and opened her business in 1872. Records of her early life are sketchy, but by the 1860s she was living in Louisville, Kentucky, and working as a lady of the evening. She had a fourteen-year-old son; he remained in Louisville, either in a boarding school or a private home, when she left for Memphis. For the rest of her life, she supported him financially. By 1876, she had moved from a more modest location into the spacious brick house on Gayoso Street, which she completely redecorated in lavish style. With its gaslight fixtures, water closets, and indoor water taps, the building was probably brighter and more comfortable than most of the buildings used as hospitals during the epidemic.[10]

Lorena Meade, who tended Cook as she lay dying, stayed at the Mansion House through the autumn until the epidemic ended. Before taking up residence under Cook's roof, Meade had lived with four other women. The 1870 census listed the occupations of all five women as "bawd." She did not contract the fever, although she tended many patients and stayed with Cook constantly during her illness. In a tribute to Meade's loyalty, newspaper editor J. M. Keating wrote that there were "bodies in the potter's field she dressed for their narrow home" and "convalescents walking the streets today, who speak her name with gratitude and veneration."[11]

Captain James Lee, founder of the famous Lee Line of steamboats, weathered the epidemics and the other ups and downs of nineteenth-century Memphis. Born in rural Tennessee 1808, Lee worked on riverboats on the Cumberland River as a young man. By the early 1840s, he was captain of the *Old Hickory*, which stopped at Memphis on its way from Nashville to New Orleans. In the 1850s he settled in Memphis, where he ran newspaper ads billing himself as one of the oldest and best commanders on the western rivers. After the Civil War, he founded a line of steamboats, of which the most famous was the *Robert E. Lee*. For many years, even with stiff competition from the railroads, the boats of the Lee Line carried planters' supplies and cotton in and out of the city.[12]

Lee was a big man, weighing more than three hundred pounds, and his legs were weak from being scalded in a boiler explosion. Local craftsmen made special chairs for him out of hickory wood, and he used them when he sat on the promenade deck of his boats, shouting orders to his crew or greetings to passing fishermen. His valet, Sam, brought him mint juleps, and a lady admirer sent bouquets from her garden for the captain's table. He spent most of his time on one boat or another, surrounded by men who listened to his colorful stories. At mealtime, he would announce that he needed to "get the wrinkles out" of his big belly. Everyone on his boats ate well, and cooks outdid themselves in order to hear him brag about the dishes served at his table. Some of his favorites were Mississippi River catfish, saddle of mutton, and green-apple pie. After dinner, he entertained anyone who would listen with improper jokes and long, involved stories of Davy Crockett, Andrew Jackson, and the old days in Tennessee.[13]

His best days were behind him when he became captain of the brand new steamer *Phil Allen*, built in the early 1870s by Primus Emerson. At the age of sixty-three, Lee admitted that his legs would no longer carry his big body up and down the steps from one deck to the other, and his business was also declining. In the 1870s and 1880s, railroads took over the lion's share of both the passenger and the freight business, and in the 1880s barge lines began displacing the old packet boats. Lee and his sons could not compete on the long runs between Memphis and St. Louis or Memphis and New Orleans, and so they turned their attention to short hauls to Cairo and to Friars' Point, Mississippi. In 1887, when he was nearly eighty years old, Lee left the river and relinquished his business to the younger generation.[14]

Samuel Stacker Lee, the son of the old captain, became a legend on the river. During the Civil War, sixteen-year-old Stacker had left home and joined the Confederate cavalry. The old captain's valet, Sam, rode with the young man and loved telling war stories. After the war, young Lee became a clerk on the *Phil Allen.* By 1879, he had worked his way up to captain on a new boat named the *James Lee.* In May of 1882, the *James Lee* won a race against five other boats from Helena, Arkansas, to Memphis, beating by an hour and twenty-nine minutes the time of the *Robert E. Lee* in its great race against the *Natchez* in 1870. With the help of his family, Stacker kept the Lee Line in business until 1925, long after the heyday of the steamboats had passed.[15]

On one of his short hauls, Stacker Lee had to control a passenger who suffered a case of delirium tremens (DTs). The man went crazy, and deckhands had to prevent him from jumping overboard. When he came to his senses, Lee told him that he had gone into the river and, without the intervention of one of the crew, he would have become "a mermaid's sweetheart or some other water fowl." Lee ordered the drunkard to go to bed and stay there until they reached Friar's Point. "The hell," said the man, "if all that happened, how the hell did my clothes get dry so quick?" Lee explained that the man's clothes were so oily that water would not stick to them. The man mulled this over for a moment and then said, "Stack, I guess you had better give me a stateroom and put one of the bellboys at each door so I can't get out again."[16]

Stacker Lee had a wild side that endeared him to rivermen and made his name a part of American folklore. Deckhands and roustabouts had heard the stories of his exploits as a boy-soldier in the Rebel army. They admired him for working his way up from clerk to captain. When his father wanted him to settle down and get married, Stacker balked. He liked the ladies and had a reputation as a tomcat, and the rivermen loved him for that, too. Sometime in the 1880s or 1890s, roustabouts started singing a song about Stacker Lee known variously as "Stagger Lee" or "Stag-o-Lee." Entertainers began singing it in waterfront saloons, and eventually, the song became associated with a man named Lee Shelton, also known as "Stag" Lee Shelton, who shot a man in a St. Louis saloon in 1895. But many people in Memphis continued to connect it to Stacker Lee, the riverboat captain.[17]

Another man named Lee became a local hero on May 8, 1925, when he rescued passengers from the capsized steamboat *Norman.* Tom Lee, an African American levee worker, gathered victims into his small open boat and transported them from the main channel of the Mississippi to the bank of the river. He mounded sand on some of the shivering people to keep them warm, while he returned to fill his boat a total of four times. In all, he rescued thirty-two people from the disaster. Seventeen others swam ashore, and twenty-three died. The people onboard the *Norman* were members and guests of the Engineers Club of Memphis on an inspection tour of flood-control structures. Grateful club members, with help from the Memphis *Commercial Appeal,* raised money to buy and repair a small house for Lee and his wife. Lee passed away in 1952, and two years after his death, the city erected a monument to his heroism in a park they named Tom Lee Park. When a storm destroyed the monument in 2003, the city developed Tom Lee Plaza with a statue of Lee saving a drowning man.[18]

Memphis's most enduring legacy is the music created in the city by artists like W. C. Handy. For Handy and other African American artists and entertainers, the city's attractions included its large black population, strong ties to the rural South, thriving black middle class, exhilarating night life, and connections by water and rail to the urban cultures of New Orleans and St. Louis. In 1899, when the city's recreational facilities barred black residents, a successful African American businessman named Robert Reed Church constructed a landscaped park with a theater, bandstand, and refreshment counters on the east end of Beale Avenue (later known as Beale Street). Between Church's Park on the east and the Mississippi River levees on the west flowed a constant stream of shoppers, businessmen, pleasure-seekers, tough guys, and lawbreakers, surging in and out of insurance agencies, barber shops, doctors' and dentists' offices, music and clothing stores, restaurants, saloons, and semi-secret alleys that barely concealed gambling dens and brothels. This street became the inspiration for much of Handy's music, including his popular "Beale Street Blues."[19]

One of Handy's favorite hangouts on Beale Street was Pee Wee's Saloon, a kind of headquarters for local musicians. In his memoirs, he described it as a place of "wistful gaiety," filled with jockeys, gamblers, dandies, and fancy women. "Mack Harris was there," he wrote, "one of the great poker players of his time. Gamblers of all complexions came from St. Louis, Chicago, Philadelphia and New York to take a hand with him and find out for themselves whether or not he was as good as his reputation." Musicians would check their instruments and stack them in the back room in hopes of getting a telephone call offering them jobs. Handy wrote some of his songs while leaning on Pee Wee's cigar stand.[20]

Before he won fame as a composer, Handy supplemented his income by playing with his dance orchestra on Memphis-based excursion boats. In 1909, he and his talented band played on the small steamer *Pattona* when it escorted President Taft's vessel into the Memphis waterfront. During that same year, Handy composed a song called "Mr. Crump" as campaign music for Edward H. Crump, who was running for mayor of Memphis. Several years later, he arranged the piece and retitled it "The Memphis Blues." In the meantime, he continued performing on the *Pattona* for fees that ranged from seven to fifty dollars for shows that could last an entire day and night. His musical skill and genial personality made him a popular entertainer and helped him to support a wife and family.[21]

In the autumn of 1914, at the age of forty-one, Handy composed his most famous song, "The St. Louis Blues." Years later, he recalled the circumstances that inspired him. Distracted by his boisterous family, he rented a room near Beale Street, where the sounds from saloons and pool halls hummed in the background as his mind drifted back twenty years to a time when he was broke, out of work, and dejected on the St. Louis levee. The memory of an inebriated woman moaning about her hard-hearted lover set the mood and provided the specific content for the song. From that recollection, his mind wandered to his experiences in the rural South, listening to the sing-song intonations of dance callers and preachers and the musical phraseology of workers in the cotton fields, and those influenced the tone and the melody. Lights flickered on Beale Street as he wrote the opening line, "I hate to see the evening sun go down," but again, he was thinking back to the time when, homeless and jobless, he "had to sleep on the cobbles down by the river in St. Louis." He had a roof over his head when he wrote this song, but the river was not far from his door.[22]

In the 1920s, after Handy had moved on to New York and national fame, Memphis still hoped for a return to the glory days of Captain James Lee and the riverboats, but the river changed, and time moved on. River currents constantly deposited silt in front of the city, creating an island of mud. The Corps made valiant efforts to control the contours of the

Mississippi, but the river kept asserting its power. Levee breaks in the spring of 1927 unleashed a torrent that flooded millions of acres of land between Cairo and the Gulf of Mexico. In response to this disaster, the Corps constructed a monumental system of levees and floodways that protected Memphis and other cities and made the river more navigable for tugboats and barges but turned passenger boats, gamblers, and captains like Jim and Stacker Lee into romantic ghosts.[23]

Beale Street changed, too. Thirteen-year-old Elvis Presley arrived in Memphis with his family in 1948, and he eventually found his way to the famous thoroughfare, but the street had become seedier and more ominous after dark. Pawnshops and liquor stores had begun to displace doctors' and dentists' offices, although the street was still lined with drugstores, diners, gambling dens, theaters, clubs and saloons, and bordellos were still discreetly hidden on side streets. Parts of the area were danger zones, where whites could not venture without permission from local gang leaders. Elvis lived in a federal housing project and attended a public high school. He found his way to Beale Street's music stores in daylight, but he did not become a familiar figure in the bars and nightclubs until after he released his first record, "That's All Right," in 1954. In the meantime, he learned about African American music by listening to local radio station WDIA, which featured legendary artists like B. B. King and Mahalia Jackson.[24]

Elvis's style of music owed a great deal to his exposure to Beale Street. When he came to Memphis from Tupelo, Mississippi, he was a quiet country boy whose parents were affectionate but desperately poor. In high school, he did not stand out academically, but he adopted an urban "greaser" hairstyle that set him apart from his short-haired classmates. Beale Street, even in the daytime, must have been a liberating environment, and all around it, after sundown, the sound of its music throbbed in the air. As Elvis developed his performing style, he kept some of his rural roots, especially his gentle attachment to religion, but he also embraced an urban sense of personal freedom in his dress and the hip-swinging motions that excited and scandalized the middle-class establishment.[25]

The raw side of Memphis was visible on March 28, 1968, when civil rights leaders marched along Beale Street in support of striking sanitation workers. At the head of the procession was Dr. Martin Luther King Jr., who had recently addressed a huge crowd in a Memphis church and stated that "the person who picks up our garbage is just important as the physician. For if he doesn't do his job, disease is rampant." Just a few minutes after the march began, a few dozen young men broke from the ranks of the protesters and began smashing store windows and stealing shoes, stereos, and musical instruments. King's close associates led him away, commandeered a car, and took him to a Holiday Inn on the river. Police came rushing in with guns, nightsticks, and tear gas, arresting some of the marchers, injuring others, and fatally shooting a young black man.[26]

In his motel room about five blocks from Beale, King passed a terrible night, feeling that he had caused the death of a young man. Late the next morning, local leaders came to the room and apologized to him. He talked with them and promised to lead another march that would be completely peaceful. In recorded conversations he told associates that he was afraid that this violent episode threatened the larger movement of which he was the guiding force. During the next few days he flew to his home in Atlanta, spoke with his wife and friends, and made plans to return to Memphis despite his own deep sense of foreboding. On Sunday, March 31, he delivered a sermon at the National Cathedral in Washington, DC. It would be his last. The following Wednesday, April 3, he flew back to Memphis.[27]

This time he stayed in the Lorraine Motel, a black-owned establishment that was a haven for musicians. At the motel, federal marshals handed him an injunction against the planned march. That evening, in the middle of a thunderstorm, he spoke to a large crowd, telling them that, in spite of death threats, he would not back down. He had no idea what would happen to him, but it did not matter, he said, "Because I have seen the mountaintop." He might not live much longer. But he said he was happy, because "Mine eyes have seen the glory of the coming of the Lord." The applause was thrilling, and King stayed with the crowd for a long time, shaking hands.[28]

On the following afternoon, he was getting ready to go to dinner and a rally. While colleagues milled around in the courtyard, King stepped out on the balcony of the motel. He called down and said he was ready to go. At about six o'clock, staff members heard a sharp sound, like a firecracker. He fell backward with his feet pressed against the railing. The first to reach him was a Memphis policeman, who tried to stop the bleeding with a towel. Friends came to his side. People in the courtyard screamed and wept. An ambulance took King to the hospital, where he died an hour later. Lorraine Bailey, the proprietor of the motel, had a stroke that evening and died four days later.[29] After King's assassination, Memphis and Beale Street fell on hard times. Riots broke out, not only in Memphis, but in other American cities.

In 1970, the Memphis Housing Authority began razing many of the commercial buildings on Beale Street and residential buildings on adjacent streets in a misguided effort to save the urban core. The site of Pee Wee's Saloon became a vacant lot. The wrecking ball spared a statue of W. C. Handy that had been erected in 1931 on a small plot of land called Handy Park, but the real W. C. Handy, who died in 1958, would scarcely have recognized the street he had memorialized in song.[30]

"Beale Street Blues" was a sad song that took into consideration the gritty side of Memphis's history and the edgy reality of Beale:

> You'll see pretty Browns in beautiful gowns,
> You'll see tailor-mades and hand-me-downs,
> You'll meet honest men and pickpockets skilled,
> You'll find that business never closes until somebody gets killed.

But the song ended with a heartfelt wish: "I'd rather be here than any place I know."

CHAPTER FOURTEEN

Musicians and Entertainers

The showboat *French's New Sensation*
From the Collection of the Cape River Heritage Museum, Cape Girardeau

By six o'clock a stir—a little electric unrest—an undercurrent of excitement could be sensed aboard the show boat. They came sauntering back from the woods, the town, the levee. They drifted down the aisles and in and out of their dressing rooms. Years of trouping failed to still in them the quickened pulse that always came with the approach of the evening's performance.

—Edna Ferber, *Show Boat*

Music and theater were part of river life from the earliest days of steamboating. Chapman's Floating Theater, built in Pittsburgh by William Chapman, with an auditorium that seated two hundred, began plying the Ohio and the lower Mississippi rivers in 1831. In 1856, a Massachusetts inventor named Joshua C. Stoddard gave the world the raucous calliope, a keyboard instrument that created sound by pushing steam through a series of whistles. Within a few years, most riverboats carried either a calliope or a brass band to entertain passengers and lure townspeople to the landings.[1]

The Civil War drove showboats from the river, but the late nineteenth and early twentieth centuries brought a renaissance of river entertainment. Beginning in 1878, Augustus Byron French's *New Sensation* brought true variety to audiences up and down the Ohio and lower Mississippi. French's troupe included singers, comics, burlesque and sleight-of-hand performers, acrobats, aerialists, and contortionists. Ralph Waldo Emerson (Gaches), the "Showboat King," operated several floating theaters, including the famous *Cotton Blossom,* in the first half of the twentieth century. He sold an equally well-known boat, the *Goldenrod,* to Captain J. W. (Bill) Menke of St. Louis, whose career, as we will see, would span more than six decades.[2]

A typical Mississippi River showboat consisted of two parts: a floating theater on a barge and a steamboat that pushed it up and down the river. Power came from the engine rooms in the steamboat, but the pilothouse rested atop the boxlike theater on the flat-bottomed barge. Long tiller lines ran from the pilothouse to the rudders on the steamboat, and the two boats were fastened together with chains. The crew of the steamboat included an engineer, a fireman, deckhands, cabin boys, and at least one cook. There were living quarters for actors and crew on the steamboat.[3]

The auditorium took up a large portion of the space on the floating theater. Usually, there was a main deck and a balcony. In front of the main deck was a ticket office. Porches and walkways provided space for people waiting in line to buy tickets or mingling during breaks in the performances. The stage was located at the rear of the auditorium, and behind it were dressing and prop rooms. When it neared a town, the steamboat blew its whistle to announce the approach of the showboat, and in the evening, it provided a great spectacle of electric lights.[4]

The din of the calliope drew audiences. Riverboat captain John Streckfus knew the value of this cacophony. When Streckfus's son Joseph (Joe) left for college, his father told him not to come home until he had learned to play twelve pieces on the calliope. The old riverboat captain knew that his business was about something more than transportation, and eventually every boat in his line had a calliope, making music that could be heard for miles up- and downstream. He knew that the sound of that instrument brought people out onto the wharves and levees and made them crane their necks to see the riverboat coming to their town. His son knew this, too, and when he returned from college for the summer, he had mastered a dozen tunes, including his favorite, "My Alamo Love." He never went back to school. His father hired him as a ticket taker and calliope player on one of his boats.[5]

In 1915, the old captain moved the general offices of the Streckfus Line from Rock Island, Illinois, to St. Louis, and strove to bring music to the river. By this time, railroads had reduced both the passenger and the freight business on the Mississippi, but the captain believed that the excursion trade would help his company survive. In 1917, he converted the side-wheeler *St. Paul* into an excursion boat operating from the St. Louis levee. Advertisements proclaimed that the luxurious vessel had three roomy decks, five thousand lights, one thousand electric fans, and the best dance music on the Mississippi. By 1920, he had rebuilt three other steamers and named them the *J. S. Deluxe*, the *Capitol*, and the *Washington*. His sons continued running the excursion business after the old captain's death in 1925.[6]

Entertainment was a key feature of all the Streckfus excursions, and the *J. S. Deluxe* became known as the "*J. S. Music.*" The old captain, who played the violin, expected his sons (Joe, Roy, John, and Verne) to master musical performance as well as navigation, boat design, and cooking. His daughter Lilly played the calliope on numerous excursions. Joe, an accomplished pianist, had a greater appreciation for music than did his siblings. In 1907, Captain John hired a young black musician named Fate Marable, who brought a new kind of dance band to the Streckfus Line. At the captain's request, Marable mastered the calliope, but he was also an excellent piano player. Every spring he gathered some of the best jazz musicians he could find to come with him to St. Louis. Within ten years, Marable had organized an orchestra that became famous, not only on the river, but around the country.[7]

Born in Paducah, Kentucky, in 1890, Marable was only seventeen when he signed on with Streckfus. His mother, Elizabeth, had taught him to play the piano and read music. Fate had reddish hair and pale skin with a smattering of freckles. When Streckfus encountered him, he was shining shoes in Paducah. A friend told him that the captain might hire him, and so he went down to the riverfront and announced that he was a pianist.

Soon he convinced his employer that he was a serious musician. In 1916, he produced his first and only published composition, "Barrel House Rag," co-authored with Clarence Williams of New Orleans. He played in jam sessions with the great jazz musicians of the era and won their respect.[8]

In 1918, Marable assembled an all-black orchestra that went down in history. From 1919 to 1921, the band known by several names, including Fate Marable and the Cotton Pickers and Fate Marable's Society Syncopators, played excursion boats out of St. Louis. At first, local audiences were skeptical, but when the band played Handy's "St. Louis Blues," the crowds went wild. The ensemble included famous names and then unknown but outstanding players like Warren (Baby) Dodds on drums, George (Pops) Foster on string bass, David Jones on mellophone, Johnny St. Cyr on banjo, Sam Dutrey on clarinet, Joe Howard on trumpet, Johnny Dodds on clarinet, and William (Bebe) Ridgely on trombone. The star of the group was a young horn player named Louis Armstrong. Marable described him as a "satchel-mouthed" trumpeter, and eventually he became known as "Satchmo."[9]

Marable's group played a kind of jazz that was especially adapted to the riverboats. The dance floors were enormous. On the *St. Paul*, as many as fifteen hundred couples could dance at the same time. Customers often congregated in front of the bandstand, but bouncers moved them along in a circular motion. The music had to be loud and lively, and the musicians followed strict arrangements. There was little chance for improvising. One observer noted that Marable knew what note each member of his orchestra was going to play next. The Streckfus family demanded music with a regular beat and a quick but not hectic tempo. They did not want to encourage wild gyrations or slow grinding music on the dance floor. Their boats were "clean" boats with no gambling or other dissipations tolerated.[10]

After Satchmo and other band members left in 1921, Marable reorganized the band and continued playing on the Streckfus Line until he retired in 1940. In 1924 his Society Syncopators recorded the famous St. Louis ballad "Frankie and Johnny" about a woman who shot the man who "done her wrong." On the flip side of this record was "Pianoflage," a novelty ragtime composition. This was the only recording Marable ever made. While Armstrong reached a worldwide audience as a recording artist, Marable remained connected to the river as a band leader, pianist, and calliopist. During the last several years of his life, he played supper

The *Admiral*
From the Collection of the Cape River Heritage Museum, Cape Girardeau

clubs in St. Louis. He died of pneumonia in 1947 at the age of fifty-six. Armstrong returned to St. Louis in 1963 to play at a fund-raiser for the St. Louis Symphony onboard the Streckfus Line's *Admiral.*[11]

Many musicians got their starts on excursion boats that moved up and down the river playing day-long engagements or one-night stands. Raymond "Peg" Meyer, a musician who grew up in Cape Girardeau, remembered the "unbridled gladness" these vessels brought to river towns. "The first thrill," he recalled in his memoirs, "was always the enchanting strains of the calliope floating over the city like echoes from outer space." The magnetic sound drew crowds of people to the waterfront. The calliope brought the crowds, but the orchestra kept them on the boat until all hours of the night, "dancing, prancing, and romancing to the sounds of riverboat jazz."[12]

In 1921, Meyer and his friend Jesse (Jess) Stacy got the chance to become part of the orchestra onboard the *Majestic.* Stacy, a gifted pianist, had to double as a calliope player. His friend remembered that the steam from the calliope blew back on the player, so he had to wear a raincoat. The metal keys got so hot that he had to wear gloves, and the sound was so loud that he had to stuff his ears with cotton. At the age of seventeen, Stacy was willing to put up with all this for the chance to learn his craft, meet other musicians, and have free transportation to the big cities along the river.[13]

For Stacy, playing music on the riverboat was a way out of poverty. His first home was a converted railroad boxcar in Bird's Point, Missouri. His father, Frederick Lee Stacy, earned his a living by ferrying railroad cars back and forth across the river from Bird's Point to Cairo. His mother moved with him to Malden, Missouri, a few months after he was born. There he learned to play piano by ear. When the family moved to Cape Girardeau in 1918, he had the opportunity to take formal lessons from music professor J. Clyde Brandt. He and Meyer formed a band for high school dances, and while they were still in their teens, they went to work on the river. By 1925, Stacy made it to Chicago, and from there he went on to New York, where he played in the Benny Goodman orchestra. In 1938, he played a memorable solo in "Sing, Sing, Sing" during a famous Goodman concert at Carnegie Hall.[14]

Meyer remembered one night in St. Louis when he and Stacy had some time off. They went to the Streckfus boat *St. Paul* to hear the young cornet player with the Marable orchestra. This was the best excursion boat orchestra he ever heard. Marable played the piano and directed the musicians from his seat, rising up from the piano bench for the crescendos. Meyer was only sixteen, and Satchmo must have been about twenty years old, but he had already perfected his craft. The young saxophone player from Cape Girardeau never forgot the experience.[15]

On all-day excursions, the musicians played about twenty minutes out of each hour. In the evening, they played 45-minute sessions with 15-minute intermissions. On the Sunday before Labor Day in 1921, the *Majestic* left St. Louis at seven o'clock in the morning with a capacity crowd heading for Ste. Genevieve. The trip downriver was uneventful, but on the way back the boat got stuck on a sandbar. In order the keep the passengers occupied, the orchestra played on and off until four o'clock the next morning, when the boat finally made it back to St. Louis. Meyer remembered that his saxophone reed had worn all the skin off his lower lip.[16]

Working on excursion boats provided an education for young Meyer. During Prohibition, alcohol was banned from the boats, but many passengers came onboard already inebriated. Some of them spent the evening sick or passed out in the restrooms. Crew members used clubs to break up fights among drunkards. Cigarettes were forbidden on the wooden boat, but many people chewed tobacco. Meyer tried it once and was sick for three days. There were lazy times, traveling from one town to the next, when musicians had time to write letters to young women. As soon as the boat arrived at a town, an employee hurried to the post office to pick up the mail. Some young men really did manage to find a girl in every port.[17]

River life could be lonely. Meyer remembered that the captain of the *Majestic* adopted a kitten that wandered up the gangplank at Chester. The stout, swaggering man would sit for long periods with the kitten resting on his belly. He brought his pet to the dinner table and allowed it to eat from his plate. After the kitten disappeared, the captain offered a reward to anyone who would tell him what had happened to the animal. No one came forward. The captain flew the flag at half-mast for several days.[18]

In 1922, Meyer left the river and returned to Cape Girardeau, where he continued to play dance music. His orchestra played in hundreds of halls in southeastern Missouri and southern Illinois. In April 1924, his orchestra played on the Eagle Packet Company's brand-new steamer *Cape Girardeau* on its maiden voyage. By 1927, the grueling schedule and hectic life of a traveling band leader no longer appealed to him, and he decided to settle down. After he left the jazz band business, he opened a music store and provided instruments, advice, and education to many school bands and young musicians. In his later years, he sold the store, but remained on its staff as an instrument repair technician. But he never forgot his experiences on the riverboats.[19]

One man who never left the river was John W. "Billy" Menke, the showboat impresario. Born in Cincinnati to a family of watchmakers, Menke first dreamed of going to sea. In 1902, he went to work in Jersey City, New Jersey, with his brother Ben in a watch factory. When they left their jobs at five in the afternoon, the brothers headed for the boatyard and worked there until midnight. Within two years they had built a boat and named it the *Cincy*. Instead of heading out to sea, they sent the boat by rail to Pittsburgh and floated down the Ohio River to their hometown. A friend of theirs talked them into showing a motion picture on their boat, and on New Year's Day 1904 they took the show down the river. Two weeks later, the Menke brothers were ice-bound at Uniontown, Ohio, where they spent the rest of the winter fishing and doing odd jobs. When spring came, the owner of *French's New Sensation* hired the two eager young men and their boat as an advance team to promote his floating entertainment. That was the beginning of Menke's career.[20]

Within two decades, Billy Menke owned several showboats, including the *Hippodrome*, the *Sunny South*, *French's New Sensation*, and the *Goldenrod*. In 1914, he and a business partner took the *Hippodrome* out onto the ocean. Broke and bored in Louisiana, they chugged out through Lake Ponchartrain and the Mississippi Sound to Mobile Bay. Storms and fog plagued them on this journey, and Menke vowed never again to go out to sea in a showboat. During the boom years of the 1920s, Ben Menke commanded the *New Sensation* with another sibling, Charley, as first mate. Billy took charge of the *Goldenrod* with a fourth Menke brother, Harry, as his right-hand man. In 1927, Menke told a reporter that if he sold his boats he would never have to work again, but he would not sell them. "Where else would I get the fun, the adventure of this life?"[21]

Wherever he went on the *Goldenrod*, he made a dramatic entrance. Placards on barns and corn cribs announced the "World's Biggest Showboat." Whistles blew as the boat nosed into the landing, where crowds of people came to greet the players. No one in town could sleep through the sounds of the calliope in the early morning. By evening, the boat vibrated with excitement as actors applied their makeup while men, women, and children filed up the gangplank and into a theater with 1,250 plush red seats.[22]

Menke's actors performed in a variety of plays, mostly melodramas, including "Over the Hill to the Poorhouse," "The Convict's Daughter," and "Uncle Tom's Cabin." His casts included vaudevillians with a variety of musical talents and straight dramatic actors from stock and repertoire companies. Performers who went on to successful careers included the comedian Red Skelton and television actress Kathleen Nolan. The showboat was a good training ground. Straight players had to participate in musical numbers between acts. Actors often played more than one role in the same production, and everyone had to pitch in, taking tickets, handing out flyers, or playing in the orchestra. Life on the boat could be pleasant, with shows every evening and free time during the day. Salaries were small, but food and living quarters were free.[23]

In the 1920s, Menke's wife and young daughter mingled on the boat with an ever-changing ensemble of players. During the long days, the women of the company worked on their costumes, did needlework, socialized, and played with the various pets onboard the boat. Men had time to loaf, fish, swim, and tell stories about their experiences in this or that production or city or town. Menke liked to talk about mishaps like the time the *Goldenrod* hit a snag, and he jumped out of bed, wrapped himself in a quilt, and plugged a leak with his own body. Smiling and gregarious as he was, he enforced strict rules against lewdness, slovenliness, and fighting. His boat was a family boat, and his shows were family shows, and that was why people in small towns loved them.[24]

Life changed for Menke in the 1930s; hard times and the proliferation of movie theaters in small towns forced him to adapt to new conditions. He traded his one-night stands at tiny river landings for longer engagements in big cities. He capitalized on nostalgic feelings about the old riverboats by staging old-time melodramas. Sophisticated crowds in St. Louis loved hissing at villains and cheering plucky heroines so much that by 1937 the *Goldenrod* had become a permanent attraction at the foot of Locust Street. In 1940, Menke modernized the boat by cutting a steel hull from a barge and attaching it to the *Goldenrod.* By that time, he was famous. Visitors, reporters, actors, and old friends from all over the world boarded the boat and sat down for long conversations in Menke's office surrounded by pictures of Walter Huston, Gertrude Lawrence, Helen Morgan, and other stars.[25]

When the musical film version of Ferber's *Show Boat* opened in St. Louis in 1951, Metro-Goldwyn-Mayer studios sent a special award to Captain Menke. Before the first showing of the movie, Captain Donald T. Wright, editor of the *Waterways Journal*, presented him with a trophy inscribed "To Capt. Billy Menke commemorating 50 years of river show-boating." Wright praised Menke's staying power and compared him to the novel's Captain Andy Hawks, who loved the river too much to leave it. "He loved her," Ferber wrote, "feared her, respected her." Cap'n Andy could never be happy except on his boat. "To leave the river—to engage, perforce, in some landlubberly pursuit was to him unthinkable."[26]

In the 1950s and 1960s, the days of the riverboats clearly were numbered. By 1953, there were only two showboats left on the Mississippi. The *Majestic* was the only one still plying the waterways; the *Goldenrod* was permanently moored in St. Louis but still offering nightly performances.

Writer Berniece Roer visited the *Goldenrod* in 1960 and was saddened by its shabbiness. She, her husband, and a visitor sat "in a listing loge upon little Victorian chairs with red plushy, moth-eaten upholstery." A black cat prowled around the aisles, and the place had a musty smell. The audience still cheered the hero and booed the villain, but Roer's mind wandered to a time in 1923, when she was a child and the *Goldenrod* docked in her town, gleaming like a jewel on the waterfront.[27]

Fire gutted the aging vessel in June 1962, but Menke insisted on rebuilding it. The eighty-one-year-old captain with a twinkle in his eye and a cigar in his mouth told reporters that the boat did not look any worse than it had in 1927 when it sank in the Ohio River. He had salvaged it then, and he intended to do it again, but the effort proved too much for him, and he sold the boat to some local businessmen. They refurbished it, and Menke continued to live in an apartment on the boat's second deck with his younger brother Charlie. In the winter, Menke liked to sit in a rocking chair near the stove, and in the summer he sat on the veranda with his gray cat, Pinky, on his lap. He enjoyed reminiscing with visitors about the boats he had owned and lost to floods and other disasters, but in his mind the *Goldenrod* was the largest, fastest, and finest of them all.[28]

Showboats and excursion boats faded away, but the music they brought to the river endured. Artists like W. C. Handy found employment on the boats and inspiration on the docks and levees. Handy, Satchmo, and other musicians and entertainers absorbed the sights and sounds of the river and placed them in the mainstream of popular culture. For Handy the sounds of the lonely riverfront in St. Louis and the crowded wharves of Memphis became the melody and the sights became the lyrics that helped define the blues.

Conclusion

The Mississippi River brought good and bad fortune to the towns and cities along its banks. St. Louis prospered by turning its back on the river, embracing industrial development, and spreading to the west. Ste. Genevieve retreated into the shadows of the limestone bluffs and remained a small town enfolding the hidden treasures of its French heritage. Chester saw the rough side of river life, becoming the site of a state prison. In Cape Girardeau, entrepreneurs embraced the riverboats as a source of wealth and a connection to the wider world. Cairo sank under the weight of its troubled history and persistent floods. New Madrid stood near the epicenter of a natural disaster in the nineteenth century and a man-made epic in the twentieth. Memphis endured plagues and tragedies and captured the soul of the river in its music.

For the people of the Mississippi valley, the twists and turns of the river meant life or death. Workers on the riverboats faced constant danger from snags, sandbars, fires, and explosions. Cholera and yellow fever spread from one river landing to another, killing thousands of people in Memphis and St. Louis and bringing contagion to every small town along the way. During the Civil War, the Union and Confederacy fought desperate battles for control of the Mississippi. Quiet little Cape Girardeau became a fortified city, and Cairo became a base for the Federal army and navy. In the aftermath of the war, the explosion on the *Sultana* heaped more misery on war-weary troops just trying to find their way home. One of the most powerful images of life on the river is that of George Robinson, escaping from the *Sultana* and floating down to Memphis on the body of a dead mule.

With luck and perseverance, river workers sometimes achieved the American dream. William Wells Brown started out as a slave working as a steward on the boats and became a well-known author and antislavery crusader. Mark Twain pursued his dream of being a river pilot long before he became a literary giant. John Henton Carter ("Commodore Rollingpin") worked in the galleys on steamboats and then made a living as a writer. Many lesser-known men rose through the ranks from cabin boy, cook, dishwasher, or deckhand to become mates, pilots, or captains. Musicians like Fate Marable and Jess Stacy escaped from poverty by traveling on excursion boats and playing with dance bands. Most famous, of course, was Louis Armstrong, who started his career in Marable's band.

For people who worked on the boats or lived on the banks, the river had a meaning beyond the struggles of daily life, beyond ambition, and beyond success. The real significance of the river was in the mind. After a long career as a captain and a string of financial disasters, "Buck" Leyhe spent his declining years in his boat store on the St. Louis wharf, musing about the Mississippi. Billy Menke lived in an apartment on his showboat and refused to leave it even after a destructive fire. Captain Don Bader spent his adult life working on a dredge boat for the Corps of Engineers. He hated to leave his family for days and weeks at a time, but he "loved his damn job." No matter how difficult it was for Bader, or any of the rivermen, to leave their families on land, they found a special kind of life on the river. The river was different every time you looked at it. The river was never the same.

Appendix One

GLOSSARY OF NAMES

Albert, Irvin—boat store owner and agent for the Eagle Packet Company
Albert, Lee—official river observer for the U.S. Weather Bureau
Armstrong, Louis—world-renowned musician who got his start on the Streckfus Line of riverboats
Arstie, William—publisher of *Waterways Journal* in the early twentieth century
Bader, Don—captain of a dredge boat for the Corps of Engineers
Bionda, Kate—riverfront snack shop owner's wife who was the first to die in the Memphis yellow fever epidemic
Bixby, Horace—pilot who trained Mark Twain
Botsh, Charley—mate who worked for the Eagle Packet Company
Brown, Charles—deckhand and outlaw
Brown, William Wells—worked as a slave in steward's department on several riverboats and later escaped slavery and became a well-known writer and abolitionist
Brown, William—pilot of the steamboat *Pennsylvania*
Carter, John Henton ("Commodore Rollingpin")—steamboat cook and baker who left the river for the writing life
Cavelier, Louis—blacksmith on the steamboat *Mandan*
Chapman, William—owner of *Chapman's Floating Theater*
Clark, George—pilot who "wore out" three towboats pulling barges piled with logs near Cairo
Clay, Charlie—cooked for President Taft on his inspection tour of the river
Clemens, Henry—Mark Twain's brother who died when the *Pennsylvania*'s boilers exploded
Clemens, Samuel (Mark Twain)—riverboat pilot who became famous as an author

Cohern, Gib—riverboat gambler

Conley, William—steamboat captain who helped a slave named Arminta to escape

Cook, Annie—madam who died nursing victims of yellow fever in Memphis

Cooper, Walter—roustabout who sued the Eagle Packet Company after he was injured

Corliss, John—one of those who died in the *Sultana* disaster

Crawford, Violet—former slave who took refuge on a flatboat near Cairo, where she met and married George Washington

Dedman, Priest (aka Crying John)—roustabout who fell overboard and drowned after a protest over wages on the Eagle Packet Company's steamer *Cape Girardeau*

Devol, George—riverboat gambler

Dodds, Johnny—jazz musician who got his start on riverboats

Dodds, Warren "Baby"—jazz musician who got his start on riverboats

Drum, Larry—Cape Girardeau man who rose from deckhand to pilot to captain

Dutrey, Sam—jazz musician who got his start on riverboats

Eads, James B.—inventor of a diving bell, builder of armored vessels for the Union, and designer of a famous St. Louis railroad bridge

Elliott, Henry—master and commander of the steamboat *Hecla*

Emerson (Gaches), Ralph Waldo—known as the "Showboat King"

Emerson, Primus—builder of armored vessels for the Confederacy

Fink, Mike—legendary flatboatman

Foote, Andrew H.—commander of Union naval forces during the Civil War

Forman, George—deckhand who wrote about brutal mates

Foster, George "Pops"—jazz musician who got his start on riverboats

French, Augustus Byron—showboat entrepreneur

Giboney, Alexander—owner of a steam-powered ferryboat at Cape Girardeau

Hall, Hubbard B.—crew member who sued the Eagle Packet Company when the watchman shot him

Handy, W. C.—composer of the "St. Louis Blues" and the "Beale Street Blues"

Hardy, George—third engineer who died when the boiler collapsed on the *Dr. Franklin 2*

Henderson, Madison—deckhand and outlaw

Hill, Mrs. Frank—cook on the towboat *Fred Nellis* when its boiler exploded and killed her

Howard, Joe—jazz musician who got his start on riverboats

Jackson, John—former slave who fueled the boilers on a Union gunboat

Jaynes, A. C.—operated a ferry service at Cape Girardeau with his sons Finis and Roy

Jeffers, Posey—riverboat gambler

Jolly, Sobieski "Beck"—river pilot who served on several Union boats during the Civil War

Jones, David—jazz musician who got his start on riverboats

Karl, Don—first mate on dredge boats

Kimball, Don—riverboat gambler

Lee, James—riverboat captain and founder of the Lee Line of vessels

Lee, Samuel Stacker—son of James Lee and a legendary character on the river

Lee, Tom—levee worker who rescued passengers from the *Norman*

Legewood, Verdell—towboat mate from Iuka, Mississippi

Leyhe, Fred—son of "Buck" Leyhe and officer in the Eagle Packet Company

Leyhe, Henry—riverboat captain, co-owner of the Eagle Packet Company, and brother of "Buck" Leyhe

Leyhe, William "Buck"—riverboat captain and co-owner of the Eagle Packet Company

Leyhe, William Jr.—son of "Buck" Leyhe and officer in the Eagle Packet Company

Linn, Lewis—physician who treated cholera patients dumped on the landing at Ste. Genevieve

Lorimier, Louis—first ferryboatman at Cape Girardeau

Mackey, Tom—riverboat gambler

Marable, Fate—one of the best-known and possibly the best of the orchestra leaders on the river

Marsh, Grant—famous Missouri River steamboatman

McIntosh, Francis—riverboat steward lynched in St. Louis

McMurty, Robert—chief engineer on the *Dr. Franklin 2* when the boiler collapsed at Ste. Genevieve

Meade, Lorena—prostitute who selflessly cared for yellow fever victims in Memphis

Menke, J. W. "Billy"—captain of the *Goldenrod* showboat

Meyer, Raymond "Peg"—Cape Girardeau musician who played with bands on riverboats

Moro, Peter—Ste. Genevieve man who supplemented his income by pulling corpses from the river

Nolan, Kathleen—television actress who got her start on showboats

Okenfuss, Carl—captain of dredge boats for the Corps of Engineers

Owens, Louis—towboat captain

Pierce, William Leigh—flatboatman who wrote about the New Madrid earthquakes

Poe, Edgar Allan (aka Poe, E. A. "Li'l Wamp")—towboat captain who retired and went to Nashville, Tennessee

Poe, Elbert L. "Wamp"—pilot and engineer from Cape Girardeau (father of "Li'l Wamp")

Powell, John—riverboat gambler

Ridgely, William "Bebe"—jazz musician who got his start on riverboats

Robinson, George—survivor of the *Sultana* disaster

Rosche, Louis—steamboat captain from St. Louis

Rozier, Ferdinand—co-owner of the steamboat *Vandalia*

Scott, Walter—captain of the *Elizabeth Ann*

Segar, Elzie Crisler—creator of the Popeye comic strips and cartoon characters

Seward, James—deckhand and outlaw

Shrodes, Samuel—captain of boats for the Eagle Packet Company

Skelton, Red—famous comedian who got his start on showboats

Smith, Charles Allen—deckhand on the *Kate Simmons*

St. Cyr, Johnny—jazz musician who got his start on riverboats

Stacy, Jess—pianist who got his start on riverboats

Stoddard, Joshua—inventor of the calliope

Strauser, Claude N.—head of the survey division for the Corps of Engineers

Streckfus, John—captain and founder of the Streckfus Line of vessels

Streckfus, Joseph—son of John Streckfus and captain of vessels that brought jazz bands to the river

Thrower, Rose Marie—cook on towboats

Warrick, Amos—deckhand and outlaw

Washington, George—crew member on the tugboat *Myrtle* servicing Union gunboats near Cairo

Appendix Two

GLOSSARY OF BOATS

AB Chambers No. 2—steamboat on which Mark Twain worked as a pilot
Admiral—one of the excursion boats of the Streckfus Line
Adriatic—Union transport vessel during the Civil War
Agnus—steamboat based in St. Louis
Aleck Scott—steamboat that docked in St. Louis with cholera-stricken passengers
Alexander Hamilton—steamboat that burned on the wharf at St. Louis
Alice—steamboat that burned on the wharf at St. Louis
Aliquippa—steamboat that collided with the *Weston* near Ste. Genevieve
Alonzo Child—steamboat on which Mark Twain served as a pilot
Alton—part of the fleet that escorted President Theodore Roosevelt down the river
Amaranth—steamboat that docked in St. Louis with cholera-stricken passengers
American Eagle—steamboat that burned on the wharf at St. Louis
Atlantic—steamboat on which gambling led to a young man's suicide
Bald Eagle—steamboat belonging to the Eagle Packet Company
Belle Isle—steamboat that burned on the wharf at St. Louis
Benton—gunboat piloted by Horace Bixby during the Civil War
Bertrand—steamboat that hit a snag and sank in the Missouri River with Horace Bixby as pilot
Black Hawk—Union gunboat during the Civil War
Blankenship—U.S. Army Corps of Engineers survey boat
Boreas #3—steamboat that burned on the wharf at St. Louis
C. E. Hillman—steamboat that transported troops and supplies for the Union during the Civil War
Cairo—Union gunboat during the Civil War
Cambria—steamboat that snagged near Ste. Genevieve

Cape Girardeau—one of three vessels of the same name belonging to the Eagle Packet Company
Capitol—one of the excursion boats of the Streckfus Line
Carondelet—armored vessel built for the Union by James B. Eads
Champlain—steamboat that snagged near Ste. Genevieve
Cincinnati—steamboat that snagged near Ste. Genevieve
Cincy—showboat built by J. W. "Billy" Menke and his brother Ben
City of Alton—Anchor Line boat captained by Horace Bixby
City of Baton Rouge—Anchor Line boat captained by Horace Bixby
Conestoga—Union gunboat during the Civil War
Corsair—steamboat that snagged near Ste. Genevieve
Corwin H. Spencer—excursion boat operating out of St. Louis
Cotton Blossom—showboat owned by Ralph Waldo Emerson (Gaches)
Cutter—steamboat that snagged near Ste. Genevieve
Delta Queen—California steamboat that raced against the *Golden Eagle*
Doctor Franklin No. 2—steamboat that suffered a boiler collapse near Ste. Genevieve
Dunkirk—steamboat that snagged near Ste. Genevieve
Edward Bates—steamboat that burned on the wharf at St. Louis
Eliza Stewart—steamboat that burned on the wharf at St. Louis
Elizabeth Ann—towboat owned by the Missouri Barge Line
Enterprise—steamboat on which William Wells Brown worked as a slave
Eudora—steamboat that burned on the wharf at St. Louis
Flora—steamboat on which Francis McIntosh worked as a steward
Fontenelle—steamboat that belonged to Captain William Conley and sank twice
Franklin—steamboat that snagged near Ste. Genevieve
Fred Nellis—towboat on which the boiler exploded
French's New Sensation—showboat on which J. W. "Billy" Menke began his career
Frolic—steamboat that burned on the wharf at St. Louis
General Brook—steamboat that burned on the wharf at St. Louis
General Jessup—steamboat that docked in St. Louis with cholera-stricken passengers
Gladys—ferryboat operating out of Cape Girardeau
Glencoe—steamer on which many passengers died of cholera
Golden Eagle—steamboat belonging to the Eagle Packet Company

Goldenrod—Captain J. W. "Billy" Menke's biggest and best showboat
Gordon C. Greene—name given to the refurbished steamboat *Cape Girardeau*
Great Republic—one of the great floating palaces on the river
Grey Eagle—Eagle Packet Company boat destroyed by ice
Hecla—steamboat owned by prominent men in Ste. Genevieve
Hindoo—steamboat that snagged near Ste. Genevieve
Hippodrome—one of J. W. "Billy" Menke's showboats
Hope—steamboat burned by Confederates but eventually rebuilt
Huntsville—steamboat that snagged near Ste. Genevieve
J. J. O'Dill—steamboat owned by Louis Rosche
J. S. Deluxe—Streckfus Line excursion boat nicknamed the "J. S. Music"
James Howard—one of the great floating palaces on the river
James Lee—Lee Line boat captained by Samuel Stacker Lee
Jay Gould—towboat piloted by Sobieski "Beck" Jolly
John Gilmore—towboat piloted by Sobieski "Beck" Jolly
Josie—steamboat belonging to the Eagle Packet Company
Kate Simmons—described in Charles Allen Smith's diary
Kennedy—U.S. Corps of Engineers dredge boat
Keokuk—steamboat that burned near Ste. Genevieve
Kit Carson—steamboat that burned on the wharf at St. Louis
Lander—steamboat that snagged near Ste. Genevieve
Lexington—Union gunboat during the Civil War
Majestic—excursion boat featured music and dancing
Mandan (1)—steamboat that sank near Vicksburg, Mississippi
Mandan (2)—steamboat that burned on the wharf at St. Louis
Marmeluke—steamboat that burned on the wharf at St. Louis
Martha—steamboat that burned on the wharf at St. Louis
Mediator—steamboat on which John Morris observed riverboat gamblers
Mendota—steamboat that snagged near Ste. Genevieve
Mississippi (1)—steamboat that snagged near Ste. Genevieve
Mississippi (2)—government steamer on which President Theodore Roosevelt traveled down the river
Moore—U.S. Army Corps of Engineers survey boat
Myrtle—tugboat that serviced gunboats at Cairo during the Civil War
Natchez—steamboat that lost a famous race with the *Robert E. Lee*

New Falls City—steamboat on which Mark Twain served as a pilot
New Jersey—steamboat that snagged near Ste. Genevieve
Norman—capsized boat from which Tom Lee rescued passengers
Oceanic—steamboat on which Louis Rosche served under Captain Horace Bixby
Oregon—steamboat that snagged near Ste. Genevieve
Pacific—steamboat on which Sobieski "Beck" Jolly served as a pilot
Palestine—steamboat on which Sobieski "Beck" Jolly served as a cub pilot
Pattona—small steamer on which W. C. Handy and his band played
Paul Jones—steamboat on which Mark Twain first met Horace Bixby
Peoria—Eagle Packet Company boat destroyed by ice
Phil Allen—steamboat built by Primus Emerson and captained by James Lee
Piasa—boat belonging to the Eagle Packet Company
Pittsburgh—Union gunboat during the Civil War
R. E. DeRussy—snagboat owned by the U.S. government
Red Rover—Union hospital ship during the Civil War
Red Wing—steamboat that burned on the wharf at St. Louis
Robert E. Lee—Lee Line vessel that won a famous race with the *Natchez*
Rubicon—steamboat that snagged near Ste. Genevieve
Ruth—steamboat that sank with the wages for soldiers in General Ulysses Grant's army
Sarah—steamboat that burned on the wharf at St. Louis
Simpson—U.S. Army Corps of Engineers survey boat
Spread Eagle—steamboat belonging to the Eagle Packet Company
St. Louis—Union gunboat during the Civil War
St. Paul (1)—steamboat that docked in St. Louis with cholera-stricken passengers
St. Paul (2)—one of the excursion boats of the Streckfus Line
St. Peters—steamboat that burned on the wharf at St. Louis
Ste. Genevieve—U.S. Army Corps of Engineers dredge boat
Sultana—steamboat that sank near Memphis when boilers exploded
Sultan—steamboat that burned near Ste. Genevieve
Sunny South—one of J. W. "Billy" Menke's showboats
Taglioni—steamboat that burned on the wharf at St. Louis
Tennessee Valley—steamboat that snagged near Ste. Genevieve
Thompson Dean—one of the great floating palaces on the river

Tyler—Union gunboat during the Civil War
Vandalia—steamboat owned in part by Ferdinand Rozier
Vanguard—towboat owned by Agri-Trans
Washington—one of the excursion boats of the Streckfus Line
Weston—steamboat that collided with the *Aliquippa* near Ste. Genevieve
White Cloud—steamboat that burned on the wharf at St. Louis
White Dawn—towboat owned by Agri-Trans
Young Eagle—small boat belonging to the Eagle Packet Company
Zebulon M. Pike—first steamboat to ascend the Mississippi above the mouth of the Ohio River

Notes

Introduction

1. Herbert Quick, *Mississippi Steamboatin': A History of Steamboating on the Mississippi and Its Tributaries* (New York: Henry Holt, 1926), 338.

2. Mark Twain, *Life on the Mississippi* (Mineola, NY: Dover, 2000), 107, 112, 117, 120, 125, 139.

3. Erik F. Haites, James Mak, and Gary M. Walton, *Western River Transportation: The Era of Early Internal Development, 1810–1860* (Baltimore: Johns Hopkins University Press, 1975), 14–15.

4. Leland Baldwin, *The Keelboat Age on the Western Waters* (Pittsburgh, PA: University of Pittsburgh Press, 1941), 186–93.

5. Haites, Mac, and Walton, *Western River Transportation*, 14–17. "Cordelling" was a term that applied specifically to Mississippi River flatboats and keelboats.

6. Haites, *Western River Transportation*, 17–18, 26.

7. Walter Havighurst, *Voices on the River: The Story of the Mississippi Waterways* (New York: Macmillan, 1964), 264; E. E. Gould, *Fifty Years on the Mississippi, or, Gould's History of River Navigation* (St. Louis: Nixon-Jones Printing, 1889), 102; Twain, *Life on the Mississippi*, 108; Oscar Winther, *The Transportation Frontier: Trans-Mississippi West, 1865–1890* (New York: Holt, Rinehart, and Winston, 1964), ch. 6.

8. Havighurst, *Voices on the River*, 264; Larry Drum, interview with the author, June 24, 2011.

9. Louis H. Hunter, *Steamboats on the Western Rivers: An Economic and Technological History* (Cambridge, MA: Harvard University Press, 1949), 442–43.

10. John Habermehl, *Life on the Western Rivers* (Pittsburgh, PA: McNary and Simpson, 1901), 8, 53–54; Thomas Buchanan, *Black Life on the Mississippi: Slaves, Free Blacks, and the Western Steamboat World* (Chapel Hill: University of North Carolina Press, 2004), 62–74; Hunter, *Steamboats*, 448.

11. Habermehl, *Life on the Western Rivers*, 8; Buchanan, *Black Life*, 54–76.

12. James T. Barrett, "Cholera in Missouri," *Missouri Historical Review* 55, no. 4 (July 1961): 346–47; Linda A. Fisher, "A Summer of Terror: Cholera in St. Louis, 1849," *Missouri Historical Review* 99, no. 3 (April 2005): 189, 198; Robert A. Sigafoos, *Cotton Row to Beale Street: A Business History of Memphis* (Memphis, TN: Memphis State University Press, 1979), 55–58. See also Patrick E. McLear, "The St. Louis Cholera Epidemic of 1849," *Missouri Historical Review* 63 (January 1969): 171–81; Khaled J. Bloom, *Mississippi Valley's Great Yellow Fever Epidemic of 1878* (Baton Rouge: Louisiana State University Press, 1993).

13. See Haites et al., *Western River Transportation*, 89–100. A good history of the engineering work on the river is Frederick J. Dobney, *River Engineers on the Middle Mississippi: A History of the St. Louis District, U.S. Army Corps of Engineers* (St. Louis: Corps of Engineers, 1977).

14. Edgar Jadwin, major general, Chief of Engineers, "Flood Control of the Mississippi River and Its Alluvial Valley" (Washington, D.C.: War Department, Office of Chief of Engineers, December 1, 1927), 6, filed in RG77, box 24, folder 7402, National Archives and Records Administration, Kansas City, Missouri; Edison Shrum, "Super Floods Raging in Wide Spread Area: *The Scott County Democrat*'s Account of the 1937 Mississippi River—New Madrid County Jadwin Floodway Disaster," with additional text, January 1994, 1–3. For a book-length treatment of the 1927 flood, see Pete Daniel, *Deep'n as It Come: The 1927 Mississippi River Flood* (Fayetteville: University of Arkansas Press, 1996).

Chapter One

1. William E. Foley and C. David Rice, *The First Chouteaus: River Barons of Early St. Louis* (Urbana: University of Illinois Press, 1983), 89–94.

2. Janet Hermann, "The McIntosh Affair," *Bulletin of the Missouri Historical Society* 26, no. 2 (1970): 125; Bonnie E. Laughlin, "Endangering the Peace of Society: Abolitionist Agitation and Mob Retaliation in St. Louis and Alton, 1836–1838," *Missouri Historical Review* 95, no. 1 (October 2000): 3.

3. Hermann, "McIntosh Affair," 126–32; Laughlin, "Endangering the Peace," 4.

4. Gould, *Fifty Years*, 102; William M. Lytle and Forrest R. Holdcamper, *Merchant Steam Vessels of the United States, 1790–1868* (The Lytle-Holdcamper List), rev. and ed. C. Bradford Mitchell (Staten Island, NY: Steamship Historical Society of America, 1975), 20; Mark Twain, *Life on the Mississippi*, 22. According to the Lytle-Holdcamper list, the boats that burned at St. Louis on May 17, 1849, were the *Alexander Hamilton*, the *Alice*, the *American Eagle*, the *Belle Isle*, the *Boreas #3*, the *Edward Bates*, the *Eliza Stewart*, the *Eudora*, the *Frolic*, the *General Brook*, the *Kit Carson*, the *Marmeluke*, the *Mandan* (built 1847), the *Martha*, the *Montauk*, the *Red Wing*, the *Saint Peters*, the *Sarah*, the *Taglioni*, and the *White Cloud*.

5. Barrett, "Cholera in Missouri," 346–47.

6. Fisher, "Summer of Terror," 207–9.

7. Joseph Mills Hanson, *The Conquest of the Missouri: Being the Story of the Life and Exploits of Captain Grant Marsh* (Chicago: A. C. McClurg, 1916), 10–15.

8. James Neal Primm, *Lion of the Valley: St. Louis, Missouri* (Boulder, CO: Pruett Publishing, 1981), 297–98.

9. Louis S. Gerteis, *Civil War St. Louis* (Lawrence: University Press of Kansas, 2004), 236, 252, 255; Primm, *Lion of the Valley*, 298–99; Mary Emerson Branch, "A Story behind the Story of the *Arkansas* and the *Carondelet*," *Missouri Historical Review* 79, no. 3 (April 1985): 317–23.

10. Primm, *Lion of the Valley*, 300–307.

11. Fred Erving Dayton, *Steamboat Days* (New York: Tudor Publishing, 1939), 352; Robert A. Hereford, *Old Man River: The Memories of Captain Louis Rosche, Pioneer Steamboatman* (Caldwell, ID: Caxton Printers, 1943), 134–35, 275.

12. Roy L. Barkhau, *The Great Steamboat Race between the* Natchez *and the* Robert E. Lee (Cincinnati, OH: Picture Marine Publishing, 1952), 18–37.

13. *St. Louis Globe-Democrat*, April 9, 1899; clippings in the Ruth Ferris Collection of River Life and Lore, Box 5, in the Herman T. Pott National Inland Waterways Library, a Special Library within the St. Louis Mercantile Library at the University of Missouri–St. Louis (Ferris Collection). For a thorough discussion of Hop Alley, see Huping Ling, *Chinese St. Louis: From Enclave to Cultural Community* (Philadelphia, PA: Temple University Press, 2004).

14. *St. Louis Post-Dispatch*, February 12, 1899.

15. *St. Louis Evening Post*, October 11, 1878; J. A. Dacus and James W. Buel, *A Tour of St. Louis, or, the Inside Life of a Great City* (St. Louis: Western Publishing, 1878), 474–77.

16. Dacus and Buel, *Tour of St. Louis*, 445–46; James Wunsch, "Protecting St. Louis Neighborhoods from the Encroachment of Brothels, 1870–1920," *Missouri Historical Review* 104, no. 4 (July 2010): 203–4.

17. Dacus and Buel, *Tour of St. Louis*, 466.

18. Theodore Dreiser, *A Book about Myself* (New York: Boni and Liveright, 1922), 100–101.

19. Julian Curzon, *The Great Cyclone at St. Louis and East St. Louis, May 27, 1896* (1896; reprint, Carbondale: Southern Illinois University Press, 1997), 17–27, 75–205.

20. Hereford, *Old Man River*, 281–84.

21. *Warsaw Bulletin*, October 22, 1942, in box 64, Ferris Collection.

22. *St. Louis Post-Dispatch*, June 6, 1905.

23. Roy L. Barkhau, *History of the Eagle Packet Company* (Cincinnati, OH: Young and Klein, 1951), 28–30.

24. Primm, *Lion of the Valley*, 455–56.

25. Martin G. Towey, "Hooverville: St. Louis Had the Largest," *Gateway Heritage* 1 (Fall 1980): 2–11. For a detailed discussion of the origins of the Jefferson National Expansion Memorial, see Tracy Campbell, *The Gateway Arch: A Biography* (New Haven: Yale University Press, 2013), 26–43.

26. *Goldenrod* Showboat, National Register of Historic Places Inventory-Nomination Form, prepared in 1967, on file at the Missouri State Historic Preservation Office, Jefferson City, Missouri; "Captain J. W. Menke's Steel-Hulled Show Boat Fleet," *Waterways Journal*, May 5, 1951; "The Only Showboat on the Move," *Waterways Journal*, December 19, 1953. See further discussion of Menke and the *Goldenrod* in Chapter Twelve.

27. B. A. Botkin, *Treasury of Mississippi River Folklore* (New York: American Legacy Press, 1955), 599–602. See also W. C. Handy, *Father of the Blues* (New York: Da Capo Press, 1991). When Handy wrote this famous song he was living in Memphis; see Chapter Twelve for more about Handy and his music.

Chapter Two

1. St. Louis Circuit Court, Case Files, Civil File no. 797, February Term 1866, "Ranney, William C., Plaintiff, vs. Steamboat Hope, Defendant," housed at the St. Louis Branch of the Missouri State Archives.

2. According to the 1850 U.S. Census, William Conley, steamboat captain, lived in Bridgeport (Fayette County), Pennsylvania, the state in which he was born about 1813. He later moved to St. Louis.

3. W. J. McDonald, "The Missouri River and Its Victims: Vessels Wrecked from the Beginning of Navigation to 1925," *Missouri Historical Review* 21, no. 3 (April 1937): 458. The 1870 U.S. Census has this information about Conley and his status and place of residence.

4. *Waterways Journal*, July 18, 1942, June 5, 1948.

5. This information is found in the U.S. Census for 1850 and 1870.

6. Hereford, *Old Man River*, 50–51; Habermehl, *Life on the Western Rivers*, 41; Mary K. Dains, "Steamboats of the 1850s–1860s: A Pictorial History," *Missouri Historical Review* 67, no. 2 (January 1973): 266.

7. Virginia S. Eifert, *Delta Queen: The Story of a Steamboat* (New York: Dodd, Mead, 1960), 58; "Captain Buck Leyhe Dies Unexpectedly on July 4," in *Waterways Journal*, July 7, 1956, 10; "Capt. William H. Buck Leyhe," in *The Work Boat* (December 1945): 28, 52, on file in box 64, Ferris Collection.

8. Barkhau, *Eagle Packet Company*, 24–27.

9. William Robert White, *Child of an Eagle: Mississippi Steamboating in Cape Girardeau, Missouri* (Cape Girardeau: Ramfre Press, 1980), 12–13; Mary F. Leyhe v. William H. Leyhe, divorce granted August 7, 1913, Cape Girardeau Court of Common Pleas, Book L, Case Number 4352, on file at the Cape Girardeau County Archive Center, Jackson, Missouri.

10. White, *Child of an Eagle*, 12; "Capt. William H. Buck Leyhe," in *The Work Boat* (December 1945): 52; *Warsaw Bulletin*, October 22, 1942.

11. *Warsaw Bulletin*, October 22, 1942.

12. White, *Child of an Eagle*, 20.

13. Ibid., 20–21.

14. Ibid., 20–21, 66. On August 12, 1912, another violent episode occurred on a boat, the *Alton*, belonging to the Eagle Packet Company. Crew members were not supposed to leave the boat until all passengers had disembarked. A crew member named Hubbard B. Hall tried to leave early, and a fight ensued. Hall was shot and wounded. He sued the Eagle Packet Company, and the St. Louis Circuit Court awarded him fifty dollars in damages. Leyhe's name was not connected with the incident, which is recorded in St. Louis Circuit Court, Hubbard B. Hall v. Eagle Packet Co., Case Number 82609, February Term, 1913.

15. Barkhau, *Eagle Packet Company*, 31; St. Louis Circuit Court, Eagle Packet Co. v. Louis Boulter, Case, no. 7302, Fall Term 1917.

16. St. Louis Circuit Court, case nos. 7302, 8358, February and April Terms, 1917.

17. *Warsaw Bulletin*, October 22, 1942, on file in box 64, Ferris Collection; Eifert, *Delta Queen*, 60; clipping from the *St. Louis Star-Times*, dated September 1949 on file in box 64, Ferris Collection.

18. *Warsaw Bulletin*, October 22, 1942; White, *Child of an Eagle*, 16; Barkhau, *Eagle Packet Company*, 38; Cape Girardeau *Southeast Missourian*, March 25, 2012.

19. The boat remained afloat as the *Gordon C. Greene*, based in Cincinnati. "Capt. William H. Buck Lehhe," *The Work Boat* (December 1945); Eifert, *Delta Queen*, 62–64.

20. Barkhau, *Eagle Packet Company*, 9; *St. Louis Globe-Democrat*, April 28, 1951.

21. Capt. William H. (Buck) Lehye, "By the Mississippi," newspaper clipping dated July 1, 1947, box 64, Ferris Collection.

22. "Capt. "Buck" Leyhe Dies Unexpectedly on July 4," *Waterways Journal*, July 7, 1956; Missouri Death Certificate no. 25099, July 5, 1956, Clippings in box 64, Ferris Collection.

23. Larry Drum, interview with the author in Cape Girardeau, Missouri, June 24, 2011.

24. Drum interview.

25. Ibid.

26. Ibid.

27. Ibid.

28. Ibid.

29. Ibid.

30. Ibid.

31. Ibid.

32. Ibid.

Chapter Three

1. Carl Ekberg, *Colonial Ste. Genevieve: An Adventure on the Mississippi Frontier* (Tucson, AZ: Patrice Press, 1996), 164, 168–73; Twain, *Life on the Mississippi*, 112.

2. Bonnie Stepenoff, Debbie Bibb, and Carla L. Jordan, "Three Mothers in Ste. Genevieve: Blending the Races, 1780–1890," *Gateway* 28 (2008): 46–47; Ste. Genevieve Constable's Records, Folders 749 and 757, Ste. Genevieve Archives on microfilm at the Ozark Regional Library in Ste. Genevieve, Missouri.

3. Stepenoff et al., "Three Mothers," 47; Lytle and Holdcamper, *Merchant Steam Vessels*, 279; 1880 U.S. Census for Ste. Genevieve, Missouri, roll 715, p. 582B, Enumeration District 132.

4. Ste. Genevieve Archives, Folder 759; Mary Rozier Sharp and Louis J. Sharp, *Between the Gabouri: A History of Ferdinand Rozier and "Nearly" All His Descendants* (Authors, 1981), 52.

5. Sharp and Sharp, *Between the Gabouri*, 52; Bonnie Stepenoff, *From French Community to Missouri Town: Ste. Genevieve in the Nineteenth Century* (Columbia: University of Missouri Press, 2006), 43, 141–42.

6. Stepenoff, *French Community*, 37–38.

7. Gottfried Duden, *Report on a Journey to the Western States of North America: An English Translation*, ed. James W. Goodrich (Columbia: State Historical Society of Missouri and University of Missouri Press, 1980), 247.

8. Stepenoff, *French Community*, 59, 60, 87.

9. Ibid., 87, 172–73.

10. Ibid., 173–74.

11. Ibid., 181.

12. Lytle and Holdcamper, list of vessels lost at Ste. Genevieve.

13. James T. Lloyd, *Lloyd's Steamboat Directory and Disasters on the Western Waters* (Cincinnati, OH: James T. Lloyd, 1856), 230; Firmin A. Rozier, *History of the Early Settlement of the Mississippi Valley* (St. Louis: G. A. Pierrot and Son, 1890), 132.

14. *Lloyd's Steamboat Directory*, 230; Rozier, *Early Settlement*, 132; Record of the Coroner's Inquest, Folder 1173, Ste. Genevieve Archives.

15. Stepenoff et al., "Three Mothers," 48.

16. Ibid., 48–49.

17. Stepenoff, *French Community*, 66–67, 99–102.

18. Ibid., 147–48; Mississippi Lime Company web page, accessed 2/21/2012.

19. *Ste Genevieve Herald*, October 18, 25, 1930; *St. Louis Globe-Democrat*, October 13, 1930.

20. *St. Louis Globe-Democrat*, October 13, 15, 1930.

21. *Ste. Genevieve Herald*, October 18, 25, 1930; *St. Louis Globe-Democrat*, October 15, 1930; Lorenzo Greene, Gary Kremer, and Antonio Holland, *Missouri's Black Heritage* (St. Louis: Forum Press, 1980), 118.

22. Scott Kerr and R. H. Dick, *An American Art Colony: The Art and Artists of Ste. Genevieve, Missouri, 1930–1940* (St. Louis: McCaughen and Burr Press, 2004), 109; James G. Rogers, *The Ste. Genevieve Artists' Colony and Summer School of Art, 1932–1941* (Ste. Genevieve: Foundation for Restoration, 1998), 13.

23. Rogers, *Artists' Colony*, 12–15; Kerr and Dick, *American Art Colony*, 110, 118–27.

24. See Charles E. Peterson, "Early Ste. Genevieve and Its Architecture," *Missouri Historical Review* 35 (January 1941): 207–33; National Park Service, *National Survey of Historic Sites and Buildings: French Exploration and Settlement*. In 1970, the Ste. Genevieve Historic District received recognition as a National Historic Landmark.

25. Dirk Johnson, "The Midwest Flooding: Flood Menaces Early French Settlement," *New York Times*, July 11, 1993; "Floods Return to Towns Hit Hard in 1993," *New York Times*, May 21, 1995.

Chapter Four

1. Quick, *Mississippi Steamboatin'*, 185.

2. Homer Bassford, "Mark Twain as a Cub Pilot: A Talk with Captain Horace

Bixby," *Saturday Evening Post*, December 16, 1899, 515, reprinted in *Twain in His Own Time*, ed. Gary Scharnhorst (Iowa City: University of Iowa Press, 2010), 8–9.

3. Ibid., 10; Mark Twain, *Autobiography of Mark Twain*, vol. 1, ed. Harriet Elinor Smith (Berkeley: University of California Press, 2010), 274–75.

4. Twain, *Autobiography*, 275–76.

5. Hanson, *Conquest*, 26–29; Grant Marsh, "Mark Twain," *St. Louis Missouri Republican*, December 8, 1878, reprinted in Scharnhorst, *Twain in His Own Time*, 13.

6. Bassford, "Mark Twain," 10–11; Hanson, *Conquest*, 27; "Mark Twain among Scenes of His Early Life," *New York Times*, June 8, 1902.

7. Hereford, *Old Man River*, 136–37.

8. M. Kesterman, "Recollections of an Ohio and Mississippi River Steamboat Pilot," *Ohio Valley History: The Journal of the Cincinnati Historical Society* 10, no. 2 (Summer 2010): 71–73.

9. Ibid., 74.

10. Ibid., 74–75; U.S. Census, 1900: St. Louis, Roll T623-895, Enumeration District 216.

11. Kesterman, "Recollections," 73.

12. *Dictionary of American Biography*, vol. 2 (New York: Scribner's, 1929), 305–6; *Waterways Journal*, July 8, 1967, box 9, Ferris Collection; *St. Louis Globe-Democrat*, August 2, 1912.

13. Twain, *Life on the Mississippi*, 34–36; *St. Louis Post-Dispatch*, August 1, 1912.

14. Bassford, "Mark Twain," 11; *Waterways Journal*, August 3, 1912; *St. Louis Globe-Democrat*, August 2, 1912.

15. *Dictionary of American Biography*, 2:305–6; *Waterways Journal*, August 3, 1912; Howard P. Nash, Jr., *A Naval History of the Civil War* (New York: A. S. Barnes, 1972), 110–12.

16. Nash, *Naval History*, 111–12; Jay Carlton Mullen, "Pope's New Madrid and Island Number 10 Campaigns," *Missouri Historical Review* 59, no. 3 (April 1965): 334.

17. Nash, *Naval History*, 114–17.

18. Ibid., 119–20.

19. Hanson, *Conquest*, 71–72; "An Eye Witness Account of the Sinking of the *Bertrand*," *S & D Reflector* (Marietta, OH: Sons and Daughters of Pioneer Rivermen, March 1976), 3, in box 9, Ferris Collection.

20. Hereford, *Old Man River*, 137–36.

21. *Dictionary of American Biography*, 2:305–6; "An Eye Witness Account of the Sinking of the *Bertrand*," *S & D Reflector* (Marietta, OH: Sons and Daughters of Pioneer Rivermen, March 1976), 3, in box 9, Ferris Collection.

22. Box 9, Ferris Collection; *Dictionary of American Biography*, 2:305–6; *St. Louis Globe-Democrat*, August 2, 1912.

23. *New York Times*, June 8, 1902.

24. *St. Louis Post-Dispatch*, August 1, 1912; *St. Louis Globe-Democrat*, August 2, 1912.

25. Box 22, Ferris Collection.

26. Jane Curry, *The River's in My Blood* (Lincoln: University of Nebraska Press, 1983), 69–70n; Obituary for Elbert L. "Wamp" Poe in Cape Girardeau, *Southeast Missourian*, September 19, 1984.

27. Curry, *In My Blood*, 258–59. Curry identifies the younger Poe only as "E. A.," but he is almost certainly the "Edgar Allan Poe" that Captain Larry Drum remembered (see Chapter Two).

28. Ibid., 263.

Chapter Five

1. Natalia Marie Belting, *Kaskaskia under the French Regime* (Urbana: University of Illinois Press, 1948), 10–11, 63–64; Clarence Walworth Alvord, *The Illinois Country, 1673–1818* (Springfield: Illinois Centennial Commission, 1920), 215–16, 406.

2. Robert P. Howard, *Illinois: A History of the Prairie State* (Grand Rapids, MI: William B. Eerdmans, 1972), 68, 116.

3. Carol Pirtle, *Where Illinois Began: A Pictorial History of Randolph County* (Donning Publishing, 1995), 29, 42–43.

4. John W. Allen, *Legends and Lore of Southern Illinois* (Carbondale: Southern Illinois University Press, 1963), 177–79.

5. "Legend of the Kaskaskia Curse," *Journal of the Illinois State Historical Society* 59, no. 3 (Autumn 1966): 289–90.

6. Pirtle, *Where Illinois Began*, 133; Jeffrey Koerber and Walter L. Brieschke, "Menard: Development of a Nineteenth-Century Prison," *Journal of the Illinois State Historical Society* 96, no. 3 (Autumn 2003): 230–34.

7. Pirtle, *Where Illinois Began*, 132; Koerber and Brieschke, "Menard," 238–39; *Cape Girardeau Southeast Missourian*, July 23, 1923.

8. Donald Clemmer, *The Prison Community* (Boston: Christopher Publishing House, 1940), 77, 274–75.

9. Ibid., 77–78.

10. Ibid., 290–92.

11. Bud Sagendorf, *Popeye: The First Fifty Years* (New York: Workman Publishing, 1979), 11–12.

12. Ibid., 11.

13. Pirtle, *Where Illinois Began*, 117; Sagendorf, *Popeye*, 13–14, 74. Elzie Segar is listed in the 1910 Federal Census for Chester, Illinois, as a fifteen-year-old male living with his parents. His World War I draft registration records give his birth date as December 8, 1894. In 1917, he was employed as a cartoonist for the *Chicago Herald*. He was exempt from the draft due to a rupture. According to the 1910 Federal Census, J. William Schuchert was born in 1858 in Chester, Illinois, and was the manager of an opera house.

14. *St. Louis Post-Dispatch*, January 18, 2004.

15. Sagendorf, *Popeye*, 20–21.

16. *New York Times*, October 14, 1938; Sagendorf, *Popeye*, 83.

17. Koerber and Brieschke, "Menard," 236; Pirtle, *Where Illinois Began*, 39.

18. Koerber and Brieschke, "Menard," 243; *New York Times*, November 1, 1952.

19. *New York Times*, November 1, 1952; Koerber and Brieschke, "Menard," 244–46.

20. *New York Times*, July 27, 1993.

Chapter Six

1. Hereford, *Old Man River*, 19–22.

2. Ibid., 22–24.

3. Ibid., 24–28.

4. Ibid., 28–30.

5. Hunter, *Steamboats*, 442–47.

6. Habermehl, *Life on the Western Rivers*, 10; Hunter, *Steamboats*, 457–58.

7. Buchanan, *Black Life*, 62–73; Hunter, *Steamboats*, 446–54.

8. Buchanan, *Black Life*, 68–74.

9. Ibid., 75–76.

10. Michael Allen, *Western Rivermen, 1763–1861* (Baton Rouge: Louisiana State University Press, 1990), 100–105.

11. Ibid., 105–7.

12. Ibid., 109–26.

13. Ibid., 193–94.

14. Thomas C. Buchanan, "Rascals on the Antebellum Mississippi: African American Steamboat Workers of 1841," *Journal of Social History* 34, no. 4 (Summer 2001): 797–803.

15. Ibid., 801–3.

16. Ibid., 804–6.

17. George Forman, "Reminiscences of a Common Boatman," ed. Michael Allen, *Gateway Heritage* 5, no. 2 (Fall 1984): 37–40.

18. Ibid., 40.

19. Ibid., 40–43.

20. Hereford, *Old Man River*, 46–50.

21. Ibid, 50–69.

22. Ibid, 69–73.

23. Charles Allen Smith, "Diary of Riverboat Deck Hand Charles Allen Smith, Kept on a Trip down the Ohio River to New Orleans and Back," dated 1885–1886, entries for November 29 and December 2, 1885, P-34, in the St. Louis Mercantile Library.

24. Ibid., January 1, 1886.

25. Edwin Rosskam and Louise Rosskam, *Towboat River* (New York: Duell, Sloan, and Pearce, 1948), 58–59.

26. Ibid., 17–18; Larry Drum interview.

27. Allen, *Western Rivermen*, 31; Rosskam and Rosskam, *Towboat River*, 13.

28. Rosskam and Rosskam, *Towboat River*, 144–45; Allen, *Western Rivermen*, 231.

29. Rosskam and Rosskam, *Towboat River*, 118, 144; Allen, *Western Rivermen*, 231; Drum interview. Historian Michael Allen spent three years as a towboat deckhand and cook.

30. Don Karl, interview with the author, July 9, 2012.

31. Ibid.

32. Ibid.

33. Ibid.

34. Ibid.

Chapter Seven

1. Felix Snider and Earl Collins, *Cape Girardeau: Biography of a City* (Cape Girardeau: Ramfre Press, 1956), 16, 255.

2. Ibid., 16–24, 211, 255.

3. Ibid., 74; *Goodspeed's History of Southeast Missouri* (1888; reprint, Independence, MO: BNL Library Service, 1978), 272–74.

4. Snider and Collins, *Cape Girardeau*, 250–52.

5. Ibid., 44–46.

6. Ibid., 48–50.

7. Ibid., 50–54; Stephen B. Oates, "Marmaduke's Cape Girardeau Expedition," *Missouri Historical Review* 57, no. 3 (July 1962): 243–47. See also Anne J. Bailey, "Texans Invade Missouri: The Cape Girardeau Raid, 1863," *Missouri Historical Review* 84, no. 2 (January 1990): 166–87.

8. Bonnie Stepenoff, "The Last Tree Cut Down: The End of the Bootheel Frontier, 1880–1940," *Missouri Historical Review* 90, no. 1 (October 1995): 62–64; Snider and Collins, *Cape Girardeau*, 203, 258–63. For a book-length biography of Louis Houck, see Joel Rhodes, *A Missouri Railroad Pioneer: The Life of Louis Houck* (Columbia: University of Missouri Press, 2008).

9. *Cape Girardeau Southeast Missourian*, September 7, 1925.

10. Thanks are due to Jennifer Rowan for primary research on Samuel J. Shrodes using census, birth, death, and marriage records and obituaries, including Shrodes's obituary in the *Southeast Missourian*, July 23, 1924, and Della Shrodes's obituary, ibid., July 12, 1930.

11. Again, thanks are due to Jennifer Rowan for research in public records, obituaries, and tombstone inscriptions in Fairmount Cemetery.

12. *Cape Girardeau Southeast Missourian*, February 12, 1923; Lee L. Albert, *Memories of Cape Girardeau and the River* (Author, undated), 59. Thanks are due to Andrew Scott for primary research on Irvin Albert in local records and newspapers.

13. Albert, *Memories*, 60.

14. *Cape Girardeau Southeast Missourian*, June 9, 1920. Local records confirm Lee Don's residence in Cape Girardeau. Ling, in *Chinese St. Louis*, has much information about Chinese immigration to St. Louis.

15. *Cape Girardeau Southeast Missourian*, June 19, 1920. City directories confirm his place of residence. Thanks are due to Sharon Sanders, librarian at the

Southeast Missourian, for help in uncovering information about Lee Don.

16. *Cape Girardeau Southeast Missourian*, June 9, 19, 1920.

17. Thanks are due to Lea Bohr for primary research on Roy Jaynes, using public records and articles in the *Southeast Missourian*, October 31, 1919; February 2, 1920; April 24, 1922; June 27, November 3, 1930; October 17, 1977; March 31, June 11, 1978; January 20, 1980.

18. *Southeast Missourian*, June 27, November 3, 1930; October 17, 1977; March 31, June 11, 1978; January 20, 1980.

19. Mary Harriet Talbut, "The Bridge the Spanned the Great Depression," *Missouri Historical Review* 88, no. 2 (January 1994): 177–80.

20. Ibid., 181–84.

21. Ibid., 185–88.

22. Albert, *Memories*, 12–14, 24, 54, 60.

Chapter Eight

1. William Edward Farrison, *William Wells Brown: Author and Reformer* (Chicago: University of Chicago Press, 1969), 18–28.

2. Ibid., 28–34.

3. William Wells Brown, *Clotel, or The President's Daughter* (New York: Macmillan, 1970), 48–49.

4. John T. Flanagan, "John Henton Carter, alias Commodore Rollingpin," *Missouri Historical Review* 63, no. 1 (October 1968): 38–43. See also James V. Swift, "From Pantry to Pen: The Saga of Commodore Rollingpin," *Missouri Historical Society Bulletin* 24, no. 2 (1968): 113–21.

5. John Henton Carter, *The Man at the Wheel* (St. Louis: Author, 1898), 87–89.

6. Ibid., 141–43.

7. Ibid., 153–55.

8. Habermehl, *Life on the Western Rivers*, 8, 53–54, 60, 63–64.

9. "Explosion on Fred Nellis," in *Waterways Journal*, October 25, 1902, 9.

10. *Cape Girardeau Southeast Missourian*, September 7, 1988.

11. Box 22, Ferris Collection; U.S. Census, 1930. Further information on Charlie, or Charles, Clay proved difficult to find.

12. Karl interview. Karl's colleague Don Bader connected Menard to the early French settler Pierre Menard of Illinois. "You know—the Menard House."

13. Rosskam and Rosskam, *Towboat River*, 73–96.

14. Ibid., 95–97.

15. Ibid., 73–96.

16. Drum interview; Edna Warren, "A Family Saga of Ol' Man River," *Waterways Journal*, September 19, 1936, 7–8.

17. Rose Marie Thrower, interview with the author, April 18, 2011.

18. Ibid.

19. Ibid.

20. Ibid.

21. Ibid.

22. Ibid.
23. Ibid.
24. Ibid.

Chapter Nine

1. The standard work on the history of Cairo is John M. Lansden, *History of the City of Cairo, Illinois* (1910; reprint, Carbondale: Southern Illinois University Press, 1976). Also very illuminating is Herman R. Lantz, *A Community in Search of Itself: A Case History of Cairo, Illinois* (Carbondale: Southern Illinois University Press, 1972). In the 1960s and 1970s, photographer Preston Ewing documented the long struggle for racial justice in Cairo. His photographs are published in *Let My People Go: Cairo, Illinois, 1967–1973, Civil Rights Photographs* (Carbondale: Southern Illinois University Press, 1996).

2. Fred W. Ash, "Submerged Ambitions," *Railroad History* 196 (Summer 2007): 8–10.

3. Lansden, *City of Cairo*, 47–49; Lantz, *Community in Search of Itself*, 20.

4. James M. Merrill, "Cairo, Illinois: Strategic Civil War River Port," *Illinois State Historical Society Journal* 76, no. 4 (December 1983): 242–43.

5. Ibid., 252–54 (also 242–56, in general); Lantz, *Community in Search of Itself*, 26–27; Ash, "Submerged Ambitions," 10–11.

6. Ronald Horstman, "The Loss of Government Greenbacks on the Steamer *Ruth*," *Missouri Historical Review* 70, no. 1 (October 1975): 87–89.

7. Charles C. Brewer, "African American Sailors and the Unvexing of the Mississippi River," *Prologue* 30, no. 4 (Winter 1998): 279–82; Steven Louis Roca, "Presence and Precedents: The USS *Red Rover* during the American Civil War, 1861–1865," *Civil War History* 44, no. 2 (June 1998): 93.

8. Roca, "Presence and Precedents," 93–94.

9. Lantz, *Community in Search of Itself*, 26–27; Brewer, "African American Sailors," 285.

10. Les Fields, "Cairo Custom House," *Illinois History* (April 1999): 46–47.

11. Lansden, *City of Cairo*, 124; Ash, "Submerged Ambitions," 11, 13, 17.

12. J. Anthony Lukas, "Bad Day at Cairo, Illinois," *New York Times Magazine*, February 21, 1971.

13. Lantz, *Community in Search of Itself*, 68–81.

14. Ibid., 76; Stacy Pratt McDermott, "An Outrageous Proceeding: A Northern Lynching and the Enforcement of Anti-Lynching Legislation in Illinois, 1905–1910," *Journal of Negro History* 84, no. 1 (Winter 1999): 61–67.

15. Lantz, *Community in Search of Itself*, 139–41; Ash, "Submerged Ambitions," 20.

16. Joe Moore's scrapbook on the 1927 flood, on file at the offices of the *Charleston Enterprise-Courier*, Charleston, Missouri; RG77, box 26, folder 7410, Records of the Office of the Chief of Engineers, St. Louis, Missouri, District, General Correspondence, at the National Archives and Records Administration,

Kansas City Branch. For a book-length treatment of the 1927 flood, see Daniel, *Deep'n as It Come.*

17. Lantz, *Community in Search of Itself,* 53–59.

18. Ibid., 62–65, 84, 160–61.

19. Ewing, *Let My People Go,* xv–xvi.

20. Ibid., 10.

21. Ibid., xxi–xxii.

22. Ibid., 3–33.

23. Lukas, "Bad Day at Cairo, Illinois."

24. Dan Barry, "Where Two Rivers Converge and Two Histories Divide," *New York Times,* May 20, 2007.

Chapter Ten

1. George Byron Merrick, *Old Times on the Upper Mississippi: The Recollections of a Steamboat Pilot from 1854–1863* (Cleveland, OH: Arthur H. Clark, 1909), 35–36; folder 749, Ste. Genevieve Archives.

2. Hunter, *Steamboats,* 260–63.

3. Dobney, *River Engineers,* 54–68; Merrick, *Upper Mississippi,* 225–28; Carl Okenfuss, interview with the author, April 30, 2012.

4. Edgar Jadwin, major general, Chief of Engineers, "Flood Control of the Mississippi River and Its Alluvial Valley" (Washington, D.C.: War Department, Office of Chief of Engineers, December 1, 1927), 6, filed in RG77, box 24, folder 7402, National Archives and Records Administration, Kansas City, Missouri.

5. Ibid.; Shrum, "Super Floods"; Marion Bragg, *Historic Names and Mississippi River* (Vicksburg: Mississippi River Commission, 1977), 3–4.

6. *Scott County Democrat,* January 28, 1937; Thad Snow, *From Missouri: An American Farmer Looks Back* (Boston: Houghton-Mifflin, 1954; reprint, Columbia: University of Missouri Press, 2012), 167.

7. Shrum, "Super Floods," 3–4; *Cape Girardeau Southeast Missourian,* January 25, 1937; *Scott County Democrat,* January 28, 1937; *Charleston Enterprise-Courier,* January 28, February 4, 11, 1937.

8. *Scott County Democrat,* March 25, 1937; Shrum, "Super Floods," 8–9. See also Bonnie Stepenoff, "Sacrificial Land: History of the Bird's Point–New Madrid Floodway in Southeast Missouri," *Illinois Geographer* 54, no. 1 (Spring 2012): 1–15.

9. For a book-length treatment of the Sharecroppers' Roadside Demonstration of 1939, see Louis Cantor, *Prologue to the Protest Movement: The Missouri Sharecropper Roadside Demonstration of 1939* (Durham, NC: Duke University Press, 1969). Also very informative is Arvarh Strickland, "The Plight of the People in the Sharecroppers' Roadside Demonstration in Southeast Missouri," *Missouri Historical Review* 81, no. 4 (July 1987): 403–16. See also Bonnie Stepenoff, *Thad Snow: A Life of Social Reform in the Missouri Bootheel* (Columbia: University of Missouri Press, 2003).

10. Ben Lucien Burman, *Big River to Cross: Mississippi Life Today* (New York: John Day, 1938), 100–101.

11. Ibid., 104–11.

12. Okenfuss interview; Don Bader, interview with the author, July 9, 2012.

13. Bader interview.

14. Okenfuss interview.

15. Ibid.

16. Ibid.

17. Ibid.

18. Ibid.

19. Bader interview.

Chapter Eleven

1. Mary Sue Anton, *New Madrid: A Mississippi River Town in History and Legend* (Cape Girardeau: Southeast Missouri State University Press, 2009), 23–25.

2. Ibid., 28–35; Conevery Bolton Valencius, *The Lost History of the New Madrid Earthquakes* (Chicago: University of Chicago Press, 2013), 68–69.

3. Valencius, *New Madrid Earthquakes*, 17–25.

4. James Penick, Jr., *The New Madrid Earthquakes of 1811–1812* (Columbia: University of Missouri Press, 1976), 15–49; Valencius, *New Madrid Earthquakes*, 42.

5. Penick, *New Madrid Earthquakes*, 50–54; Valencius, *New Madrid Earthquakes*, 42.

6. Amanda Hunter's daughter Ella married William Dawson, and the family home eventually became Hunter-Dawson State Historic Site. The family and the house are well documented in the Hunter-Dawson House, National Register of Historic Places registration form, prepared by Julie Ann Lamouria and Roger Maserang, 2012.

7. Louis S. Gerteis, *The Civil War in Missouri: A Military History* (Columbia: University of Missouri Press, 2012), 136; Anton, *New Madrid*, 192–96.

8. Gerteis, *Civil War in Missouri*, 138–41.

9. Twain, *Life on the Mississippi*, 124.

10. Ibid., 125; Anton, *New Madrid*, 148–51.

11. Leon Parker Ogilvie, "Governmental Efforts at Reclamation in the Southeast Missouri Lowlands," *Missouri Historical Review* 64, no. 2 (January 1970): 165, 168, 176.

12. Stepenoff, "Last Tree Cut Down," 62–65.

13. Ibid., 68–71.

14. Ibid., 71–72.

15. Jeff Hearne, "Beginning of LaForge," *Missouri Historical Review* 88, no. 3 (April 1994): 304–11.

16. Snow, *From Missouri*, 203–9. For more information on Whitfield and the Sharecroppers' Roadside Demonstration, see Cantor, *Protest Movement*.

17. Snow, *From Missouri*, 172–73; L. T. Berthe, *Old Man River Speaks* (Charleston, MO: Author, 1937).

18. Members of the County Courts to Honorable Orville Zimmerman, House of Representatives [June 14, 1949], and Thad Snow to Colonel L. H. Foote, U.S. District Engineer, West Memphis, Arkansas, August 6, 1949, folder 5, Snow Papers; Stepenoff, *Thad Snow*, xii–xiii.

19. "Big Oak Tree State Park Swamped by Flood," Missouri Parks Association *Heritage* 29, no. 2 (June 2011): 1, 4.

20. "Towosahgy State Historic Site," in *Exploring Missouri's Legacy: State Parks and Historic Sites*, ed. Susan Flader (Columbia: University of Missouri Press, 1992), 179–81.

21. Andrew C. Revkin, "More on Tornadoes, Floods, Climate and Risk," *New York Times*, May 4, 2011; Malcolm Gay and John Schwartz, "Anxious Eyes on a River as Flooding Threat Looms," *New York Times*, April 29, 2011.

22. A. G. Sulzberger and John Schwartz, "A Levee Breached, and New Worries Downstream," *New York Times*, May 3, 2011; "Big Oak Tree Park Swamped by Flood," Missouri Parks Association *Heritage* 29, no. 2 (June 2011): 4.

23. Scott Moyers, "The Death of Pinhook: Community Will Never Return after Flooding, Residents Say," *Cape Girardeau Southeast Missourian*, June 17, 2011; "Morehouse Cleaning Up after Spring Flooding," *Cape Girardeau Southeast Missourian*, August 24, 2011; Scott Moyers, "Buyouts of Pinhook, Morehouse among Topics of Roundtable Discussion with Senator Blunt," *Cape Girardeau Southeast Missourian*, September 2, 2011.

24. George Grugett, "The Battle for Flood Protection," *Cape Girardeau Southeast Missourian*, July 27, 2011.

Chapter Twelve

1. Herman Melville, *The Confidence Man* (London: Penguin Books, 1990), 7–155.

2. Ibid., 156–60.

3. Karen Halttunen, *Confidence Men and Painted Women: A Study of Middle-Class Culture in America, 1830–1870* (New Haven: Yale University Press, 1982), 6–7, 33–35. J. H. Green's best-known work was *Gambling Unmasked* (Philadelphia, PA: G. B. Zieber, 1848).

4. Stepenoff, *French Community*, 188.

5. *Blacklegs, Card Sharps, and Confidence Men: Nineteenth-Century Mississippi River Gambling Stories*, ed. Thomas Ruys Smith (Baton Rouge: Louisiana State University Press, 2010), 3–5.

6. Hunter, *Steamboats*, 408–9.

7. John Morris, *Wanderings of a Vagabond, an Autobiography* (New York: Author, 1873), 413–30.

8. *Blacklegs, Card Sharps*, 3–5; John M. Findlay, *People of Chance: Gambling in American Society from Jamestown to Las Vegas* (New York: Oxford University

Press, 1986), 75; "Experiences of a Gambler," *Waterways Journal*, October 24, 1896, 3–4.

9. "Experiences of a Gambler," 3–4.

10. *Blacklegs, Card Sharps*, 4–5.

11. George H. Devol, *Forty Years a Gambler on the Mississippi* (1887; facsimile edition, Austin, TX: Steck-Vaughn, 1967), 25–26.

12. Ibid., 26.

13. Ibid., 27.

14. Ibid.

15. Olivia Skinner, "Our Deep-Seated Urge to Gamble," *St. Louis Post-Dispatch*, June 19, 1961.

16. "Experiences of a Gambler," 3–4.

17. Ibid., 4; Herbert Asbury, *Sucker's Progress: An Informal History of Gambling in America* (New York: Dodd, Mead, 1938), 248.

18. "Experiences of a Gambler," 4; Asbury, *Sucker's Progress*, 248–49.

19. "Experiences of a Gambler," 4; Asbury, *Sucker's Progress*, 249.

20. "Experiences of a Gambler," 4; Asbury, *Sucker's Progress*, 249. Asbury says he ended up in Seattle.

21. "Experiences of a Gambler," 3.

22. Edna Ferber, *Show Boat* (New York: Penguin Books, 1994), xiii, 134–35. The novel was first published in 1926.

Chapter Thirteen

1. Stanley J. Folmsbee, Robert E. Corlew, and Enoch L. Mitchell, *Tennessee: A Short History* (Knoxville: University of Tennessee Press, 1969), 150, 298.

2. Thomas L. Connelly, *Civil War Tennessee: Battles and Leaders* (Knoxville: University of Tennessee Press, 1979), 17, 51, 85; Jim Miles, *A River Unveiled: A History and Tour Guide to the Campaign for the Mississippi River* (Nashville, TN: Rutledge Hill Press, 1994), 68–72.

3. James D. Lockett, "The Lynching Massacre of Black and White Soldiers at Fort Pillow, Tennessee, April 12, 1864," *Western Journal of Black Studies* 22, no. 2 (1998): 84, 87–89.

4. Alan Huffman, *Sultana* (New York: HarperCollins, 2009), 121–22, 186, 191.

5. Ibid., 191–92, 208–9, 217, 232–33

6. Mother Jones, *Correspondence of Mother Jones*, ed. Edward M. Steel (Pittsburgh, PA: University of Pittsburgh Press, 1985), xxiv–xxxviii.

7. Sigafoos, *Cotton Row*, 55–56.

8. Ibid., 56; Shields McIlwaine, *Memphis down in Dixie* (New York: E. P. Dutton, 1948), 167–71.

9. McIlwaine, *Memphis*, 171–72; Franklin Wright, "Annie Cook: The Mary Magdalene of Memphis," *West Tennessee Historical Society Papers* 43 (1989): 44.

10. Wright, "Annie Cook," 45–47.

11. Ibid., 47–51.

12. McIlwaine, *Memphis*, 187–99; J. Mack Gamble, "Memphis and the Revival

of River Traffic," *Waterways Journal* 1, no. 5 (April 1920): 33–34; "A Salty Start," *S & D Reflector* 2, no. 2 (1965): 7.

13. McIlwaine, *Memphis*, 185–95.

14. Ibid., 195–97; Sigafoos, *Cotton Row*, 79; Gamble, "Revival of River Traffic," 33.

15. McIlwaine, *Memphis*, 199–205.

16. *Missouri Republican*, December 12, 1878.

17. McIlwaine, *Memphis*, 199–200; *St. Louis Globe-Democrat*, December 28, 1895.

18. *Memphis Commercial Appeal*, July 25, 2012.

19. David Robertson, *W. C. Handy: The Life and Times of the Man Who Made the Blues* (New York: Alfred A. Knopf, 2009), 110–13.

20. Handy, *Father of the Blues*, 91–92: Robertson, *W. C. Handy*, 17.

21. Robertson, *W. C. Handy*, 116–19; Handy, *Father of the Blues*, 107.

22. Handy, *Father of the Blues*, 118–21; Robertson, *W. C. Handy*, 145, 180–81.

23. Gamble, "Revival of River Traffic," 14; Daniels, *Deep'n as It Come*, 7–11; Thomas Fauntleroy, "Flood Legislation Heartens Memphis," *New York Times*, April 8, 1928.

24. Robertson, *W. C. Handy*, 16; Glen Jeansonne, David Luhrssen, and Dan Sokolovic, *Elvis Presley, Reluctant Rebel: His Life and Our Times* (Santa Barbara, CA: Praeger, 2011), 23–24. There is a long-standing debate on the question of exactly when Elvis found his way to Beale Street. For detailed and documented information on his development as a musician, see Peter Guralnick, *Last Train to Memphis: The Rise of Elvis Presley* (Boston: Little, Brown, 1994).

25. Jeansonne et al., *Elvis Presley*, 18, 19, 64.

26. Robertson, *W. C. Handy*, 16–17; Stewart Burns, *To the Mountaintop: Martin Luther King Jr.'s Sacred Mission to Save America, 1955–1968* (San Francisco: HarperSan Francisco, 2004), 424–26.

27. Burns, *To the Mountaintop*, 426–41.

28. Ibid., 441–44.

29. Ibid., 447–51.

30. Robertson, *W. C. Handy*, 15–19.

Chapter Fourteen

1. Philip Graham, *Showboats: The History of an American Institution* (Austin: University of Texas Press, 1951), 78–79, 197.

2. Ibid., 47–48, 197; "Capt. Ralph Emerson Dies in Chicago," *Waterways Journal*, July 11, 1965.

3. Betty Bryant, *Here Comes the Showboat* (Lexington: University Press of Kentucky, 1994), 12–17.

4. Ibid.

5. *St. Louis Globe-Democrat*, April 15, 1951.

6. William Howland Kenney, *Jazz on the River* (Chicago: University of Chicago Press, 2005), 19–20; Clippings on file in box 97, Ferris Collection.

7. *St. Louis Globe-Democrat*, April 15, 1951; Dolores M. Williams, "Music on the Streckfus Steamers," *Bulletin of the Missouri Historical Society* 24, no. 3 (April 1968): 242–45; Raymond F. "Peg" Meyer, *Backwoods Jazz in the Twenties* (Cape Girardeau: Center for Regional History, 1989), 66–67.

8. Kenney, *Jazz on the River*, 38–45.

9. Williams, "Streckfus Steamers," 244–45; Kenney, *Jazz on the River*, 45–46.

10. Meyer, *Backwoods Jazz*, 66–68; *St. Louis Globe-Democrat*, April 15, 1951; Kenney, *Jazz on the River*, 45–47.

11. Williams, "Streckfus Steamers," 246; Kenney, *Jazz on the River*, 60–63; *New York Times*, January 19, 1947.

12. Meyer, *Backwoods Jazz*, 51–52.

13. Ibid., 57–58; Jerry Ford, *Dreamers: Entertainers from Small Town to Big Time* (Cape Girardeau: Southeast Missouri State University Press, 2012), 23–28.

14. Meyer, *Backwoods Jazz*, 57–58; Ford, *Dreamers*, 23–28; Kenney, *Jazz on the River*, 135–39.

15. Meyer, *Backwoods Jazz*, 53, 67.

16. Ibid., 56–57.

17. Ibid., 54–59.

18. Ibid., 61.

19. Ibid., 64, 92; Ford, *Dreamers*, 21.

20. *St. Louis Globe-Democrat*, August 21, 1927.

21. Ibid.

22. Ibid.

23. Ibid.; Waterways *Journal*, July 20, 1968.

24. *St. Louis Globe-Democrat*, August 21, 1927.

25. Ibid., July 31, 1941; Katherine Grace, "Captain Menke's Goldenrod," *Ford Times* (July 1949): 42–46; *Waterways Journal*, May 5, 1951, 8.

26. Clipping dated July 14, 1951, on file in box 71, Ferris Collection; Ferber, *Show Boat*, 37.

27. *Waterways Journal*, December 19, 1953; Berniece Roer, "Madam Goldenrod … I Knew Her When," *Heartland*, March 1960, 8.

28. *Waterways Journal*, June 9, 1962; Recollections of Ruth Ferris in box 71, Ferris Collection.

Bibliography

Note for researchers: Anyone studying life on the Mississippi River would do well to visit the Mercantile Library on the campus of the University of Missouri–St. Louis. Housed in this wonderful facility is the Herman T. Pott National Inland Waterways Library. Of particular value is the Ruth Ferris Collection of River Life and Lore. Also invaluable is the full run of *Waterways Journal* in this library. Other sources consulted included the following:

Albert, Lee. *Memories of Cape Girardeau and the River.* Author, undated.

Allen, John W. *Legends and Lore of Southern Illinois.* Carbondale: Southern Illinois University Press, 1963.

Allen, Michael. *Western Rivermen, 1763–1861.* Baton Rouge: Louisiana State University Press, 1990.

Alvord, Clarence Walworth. *The Illinois Country, 1673–1818.* Springfield: Illinois Centennial Commission, 1920.

Anton, Mary Sue. *New Madrid: A Mississippi River Town in History and Legend.* Cape Girardeau: Southeast Missouri State University Press, 2009.

Asbury, Herbert. *Sucker's Progress: An Informal History of Gambling in America.* New York: Dodd, Mead, 1938.

Ash, Fred W. "Submerged Ambitions." *Railroad History* 196 (Summer 2007): 6–21.

Bailey, Anne J. "Texans Invade Missouri: The Cape Girardeau Raid, 1863." *Missouri Historical Review* 84, no. 2 (January 1990): 166–87.

Baldwin, Leland. *The Keelboat Age on the Western Waters.* Pittsburgh, PA: University of Pittsburgh Press, 1941.

Barkhau, Roy L. *The Great Steamboat Race between the* Natchez *and the* Robert E. Lee. Cincinnati, OH: Picture Marine Publishing, 1952.

———. *History of the Eagle Packet Company.* Cincinnati, OH: Young and Klein, 1951.

Barrett, James T. "Cholera in Missouri." *Missouri Historical Review* 55, no. 4 (July 1961): 344–54.

Bassford, Homer. "Mark Twain as a Cub Pilot: A Talk with Horace Bixby." In *Twain in His Own Time*, edited by Gary Scharnhorst. Iowa City: University of Iowa Press, 2010.

Belting, Natalia Marie. *Kaskaskia under the French Regime.* Urbana: University of Illinois Press, 1948.

Berthe, L. T. *Old Man River Speaks.* Charleston, MO: Author, 1937.

Blacklegs, Card Sharps, and Confidence Men: Nineteenth-Century Mississippi River Gambling Stories. Edited by Thomas Ruys Smith. Baton Rouge: Louisiana State University Press, 2010.

Bloom, Khaled J. *Mississippi Valley's Great Yellow Fever Epidemic of 1878.* Baton Rouge: Louisiana State University Press, 1993.

Botkin, B. A. *Treasury of Mississippi River Folklore.* New York: American Legacy Press, 1955.

Branch, Mary Emerson. "A Story behind the Story of the *Arkansas* and the *Carondelet.*" *Missouri Historical Review* 79, no. 3 (April 1985): 317–23.

Brewer, Charles C. "African American Sailors and the Unvexing of the Mississippi River." *Prologue* 30, no. 4 (Winter 1998): 278–86.

Brown, William Wells. *Clotel, or The President's Daughter.* New York: Macmillan, 1970.

Bryant, Betty. *Here Comes the Showboat.* Lexington: University Press of Kentucky, 1994.

Buchanan, Thomas C. *Black Life on the Mississippi: Slaves, Free Blacks, and the Western Steamboat World.* Chapel Hill: University of North Carolina Press, 2004.

———. "Rascals on the Antebellum Mississippi: African American Steamboat Workers of 1841." *Journal of Social History* 34, no. 4 (Summer 2001): 797–806.

Burman, Ben Lucien. *Big River to Cross: Mississippi Life Today.* New York: John Day, 1938.

Burns, Stewart. *To the Mountaintop: Martin Luther King, Jr.'s Sacred Mission to Save America, 1955–1968.* San Francisco: HarperSan Francisco, 2004.

Campbell, Tracy. *The Gateway Arch: A Biography.* New Haven: Yale University Press, 2013.

Cantor, Louis. *Prologue to the Protest Movement: The Missouri Sharecropper Roadside Demonstration of 1939.* Durham, NC: Duke University Press, 1969.

Carter, John Henton. *The Man at the Wheel.* St. Louis: Author, 1898.

Clemmer, Donald. *The Prison Community.* Boston: Christopher Publishing House, 1940.

Connelly, Thomas L. *Civil War Tennessee: Battles and Leaders.* Knoxville: University of Tennessee Press, 1979.

Curry, Jane. *The River's in My Blood.* Lincoln: University of Nebraska Press, 1983.

Curzon, Julian. *The Great Cyclone at St. Louis and East St. Louis, May 27, 1896.* 1896. Reprint, Carbondale: Southern Illinois University Press, 1997.

Dacus, J. A., and James W. Buel. *A Tour of St. Louis, or, the Inside Life of a Great City.* St. Louis: Western Publishing, 1878.

Dains, Mary K. "Steamboats of the 1850s–1860s: A Pictorial History." *Missouri Historical Review* 67, no. 2 (January 1973): 265–82.

Daniel, Pete. *Deep'n as It Come: The 1927 Mississippi River Flood.* Fayetteville: University of Arkansas Press, 1996.

Dayton, Fred Erving. *Steamboat Days.* New York: Tudor Publishing, 1939.

Devol, George H. *Forty Years a Gambler on the Mississippi.* 1887. Facsimile edition, Austin, TX: Steck-Vaughn, 1967.

Dictionary of American Biography. Vol. 2. New York: Scribner's, 1929.

Dobney, Frederick J. *River Engineers on the Middle Mississippi: A History of the St. Louis District, U. S. Army Corps of Engineers.* St. Louis: Corps of Engineers, 1977.

Dreiser, Theodore. *A Book about Myself.* New York: Boni and Liveright, 1922.

Duden, Gottfried. *Report on a Journey to the Western States of North America: An English Translation.* Edited by James W. Goodrich. Columbia: State Historical Society of Missouri and University of Missouri Press, 1980.

Eifert, Virginia S. *Delta Queen: The Story of a Steamboat.* New York: Dodd, Mead, 1960.

Ekberg, Carl. *Colonial Ste. Genevieve: An Adventure on the Mississippi Frontier.* Tucson, AZ: Patrice Press, 1996.

Ewing, Preston. *Let My People Go: Cairo, Illinois, 1967–1973, Civil Rights Photographs.* Edited by Jan Roddy. Carbondale: Southern Illinois University Press, 1996.

"Experiences of a Gambler." *Waterways Journal,* October 24, 1896, 3–4.

Farrison, William Edward. *William Wells Brown: Author and Reformer.* Chicago: University of Chicago Press, 1969.

Ferber, Edna. *Show Boat.* New York: Penguin Books, 1994.

Findlay, John M. *People of Chance: Gambling in American Society from Jamestown to Las Vegas.* New York: Oxford University Press, 1986.

Fisher, Linda A. "A Summer of Terror: Cholera in St. Louis, 1849." *Missouri Historical Review* 99, no. 3 (April 2005): 189–211.

Flanagan, John T. "John Henton Carter, alias Commodore Rollingpin." *Missouri Historical Review* 63, no. 1 (October 1968): 38–54.

Foley, William E., and C. David Rice. *The First Chouteaus: River Barons of Early St. Louis.* Urbana: University of Illinois Press, 1983.

Folmsbee, Stanley J., Robert E. Corlew, and Enoch L. Mitchell. *Tennessee: A Short History.* Knoxville: University of Tennessee Press, 1969.

Ford, Jerry. *Dreamers: Entertainers from Small Town to Big Time.* Cape Girardeau: Southeast Missouri State University Press, 2012.

Forman, George. "Reminiscences of a Common Boatman." Edited by Michael Allen. *Gateway Heritage* 5, no. 2 (Fall 1984): 37–43.

Gamble, J. Mack. "Memphis and the Revival of River Traffic." *Waterways Journal* 1, no. 5 (April 1920): 33–34.

Gerteis, Louis S. *The Civil War in Missouri: A Military History.* Columbia: University of Missouri Press, 2012.

———. *Civil War St. Louis.* Lawrence: University Press of Kansas, 2004.

Gould, E. E. *Fifty Years on the Mississippi, or, Gould's History of River Navigation.* St. Louis: Nixon-Jones Printing, 1889.

Graham, Philip. *Showboats: The History of an American Institution.* Austin: University of Texas Press, 1951.

Green, J. H. *Gambling Unmasked.* Philadelphia, PA: G. B. Zieber, 1848.

Greene, Lorenzo, Gary Kremer, and Antonio Holland. *Missouri's Black Heritage.* St. Louis: Forum Press, 1980.

Guralnick, Peter. *Last Train to Memphis: The Rise of Elvis Presley.* Boston: Little, Brown, 1994.

Habermehl, John. *Life on the Western Rivers.* Pittsburgh, PA: McNary and Simpson, 1901.

Haites, Eric F., James Mak, and Gary M. Walton. *Western River Transportation: The Era of Early Internal Development, 1810–1860.* Baltimore: Johns Hopkins University Press, 1975.

Halttunen, Karen. *Confidence Men and Painted Women: A Study of Middle-Class Culture in America, 1830–1870.* New Haven: Yale University Press, 1982.

Handy, W. C. *Father of the Blues.* New York: Da Capo Press, 1991.

Hanson, Joseph Mills. *The Conquest of the Missouri: Being the Story of the Life and Exploits of Captain Grant Marsh.* Chicago: A. C. McClurg, 1916.

Havighurst, Walter. *Voices on the River: The Story of the Mississippi Waterways.* New York: Macmillan, 1964.

Hearne, Jeff, "Beginning of LaForge." *Missouri Historical Review* 88, no. 3 (April 1994): 301–16.

Hereford, Robert A. *Old Man River: The Memories of Captain Louis Rosche, Pioneer Steamboatman.* Caldwell, ID: Caxton Printers, 1943.

Hermann, Janet, "The McIntosh Affair." *Bulletin of the Missouri Historical Society* 26, no. 2 (1970): 123–43.

Horstman, Ronald. "The Loss of Government Greenbacks on the Steamer *Ruth.*" *Missouri Historical Review* 70, no. 1 (October 1975): 87–89.

Howard, Robert P. *Illinois: A History of the Prairie State.* Grand Rapids, MI: William B. Eerdmans, 1972.

Huffman, Alan. *Sultana.* New York: HarperCollins, 2009.

Hunter, Louis H. *Steamboats on the Western Rivers: An Economic and Technological History.* Cambridge, MA: Harvard University Press, 1949.

Hunter-Dawson House, National Register of Historic Places Registration Form, prepared by Julie Ann Lamouria and Roger Maserang, 2012.

Jadwin, Edgar. "Flood Control of the Mississippi River and Its Alluvial Valley." Washington, D.C.: War Department, Office of Chief of Engineers, December 1, 1927. Filed in RG77, box 24, folder 7402, National Archives and Records Administration, Kansas City, Missouri.

Jeansonne, Glen, David Luhrssen, and Dan Sokolovic. *Elvis Presley, Reluctant Rebel: His Life and Our Times.* Santa Barbara, CA: Praeger, 2011.

Kenney, William Howland. *Jazz on the River.* Chicago: University of Chicago Press, 2005.

Kerr, Scott, and R. H. Dick. *An American Art Colony: The Art and Artists of Ste. Genevieve, Missouri, 1930–1940.* St. Louis: McCaughen and Burr Press, 2004.

Kesterman, M. "Recollections of an Ohio and Mississippi River Steamboat Pilot." *Ohio Valley History: The Journal of the Cincinnati Historical Society* 10, no. 2 (Summer 2010): 71–75.

Koerber, Jeffrey, and Walter L. Brieschke, "Menard: Development of a Nineteenth-Century Prison." *Journal of the Illinois State Historical Society* 96, no. 3 (Autumn 2003): 230–39.

Lansden, John M. *History of the City of Cairo, Illinois.* Carbondale: Southern Illinois University Press, 1976 reprint of 1910 edition.

Lantz, Herman R. *A Community in Search of Itself: A Case History of Cairo.* Carbondale: Southern Illinois University Press, 1972.

Laughlin, Bonnie E., "Endangering the Peace of Society: Abolitionist Agitation and Mob Retaliation in St. Louis and Alton, 1836–1838." *Missouri Historical Review* 95, no. 1 (October 2000): 1–22.

"Legend of the Kaskaskia Curse." *Journal of the Illinois State Historical Society* 59, no. 3 (Autumn 1966): 289–92.

Ling, Huping. *Chinese St. Louis: From Enclave to Cultural Community.* Philadelphia, PA: Temple University Press, 2004.

Lloyd, James T. *Lloyd's Steamboat Directory and Disasters on the Western Waters.* Cincinnati, OH: James T. Lloyd, 1856.

Lockett, James D. "The Lynching Massacre of Black and White Soldiers at Fort Pillow, Tennessee, April 12, 1864." *Western Journal of Black Studies* 22, no. 2 (1998): 84–93.

Lukas, J. Anthony. "Bad Day at Cairo, Illinois." *New York Times Magazine,* February 21, 1971.

Lytle, William M., and Forrest R. Holdcamper. *Merchant Steam Vessels of the United States, 1790–1868.* Revised and edited by C. Bradford Mitchell. Staten Island, NY: Steamship Historical Society of America, 1975.

McDermott, Stacy Pratt. "An Outrageous Proceeding: A Northern Lynching and the Enforcement of Anti-Lynching Legislation in Illinois, 1905–1910." *Journal of Negro History* 84, no. 1 (Winter 1999): 61–67.

McIlwaine, Shields. *Memphis down in Dixie.* New York: E. P. Dutton, 1948.

McLear, Patrick E. "The St. Louis Cholera Epidemic of 1849." *Missouri Historical Review* 63 (January 1969): 171–81.

Melville, Herman. *The Confidence Man.* London: Penguin Books, 1990.

Memphis Commercial Appeal, July 25, 2012.

Merrick, George Byron. *Old Times on the Upper Mississippi: The Recollections of a Steamboat Pilot from 1854–1863.* Cleveland, OH: Arthur H. Clark, 1909.

Merrill, James M. "Cairo, Illinois: Strategic Civil War River Port." *Illinois State Historical Society Journal* 76, no. 4 (December 1983): 242–56.

Meyer, Raymond F. "Peg." *Backwoods Jazz in the Twenties.* Cape Girardeau: Center for Regional History, 1989.

Miles, Jim. *A River Unveiled: A History and Tour Guide to the Campaign for the Mississippi River.* Nashville, TN: Rutledge Hill Press, 1994.

Morris, John. *Wanderings of a Vagabond, an Autobiography.* New York: Author, 1873.

Mullen, Jay Carlton. "Pope's New Madrid and Island Number 10 Campaigns." *Missouri Historical Review* 59, no. 3 (April 1965): 325–43.

Nash, Howard P., Jr. *A Naval History of the Civil War.* New York: A. S. Barnes, 1972.

Oates, Stephen B. "Marmaduke's Cape Girardeau Expedition." *Missouri Historical Review* 57, no. 3 (July 1962): 237–47.

Ogilvie, Leon Parker. "Governmental Efforts at Reclamation in the Southeast Missouri Lowlands." *Missouri Historical Review* 64, no. 2 (January 1970): 150–76.

Penick, James, Jr. *The New Madrid Earthquakes of 1811–1812.* Columbia: University of Missouri Press, 1976.

Peterson, Charles E. "Early Ste. Genevieve and Its Architecture." *Missouri Historical Review* 35 (January 1941): 207–33.

Pirtle, Carol. *Where Illinois Began: A Pictorial History of Randolph County.* Donning Publishing, 1995.

Primm, James Neal. *Lion of the Valley: St. Louis, Missouri.* Boulder, CO: Pruett Publishing, 1981.

Quick, Herbert. *Mississippi Steamboatin': A History of Steamboating on the Mississippi and Its Tributaries.* New York: Henry Holt, 1926.

Rhodes, Joel. *A Missouri Railroad Pioneer: The Life of Louis Houck.* Columbia: University of Missouri Press, 2008.

Robertson, David. *W. C. Handy: The Life and Times of the Man Who Made the Blues.* New York: Alfred A. Knopf, 2009.

Roca, Steven Louis. "Presence and Precedents: The USS *Red Rover* during the American Civil War, 1861–1865." *Civil War History* 44, no. 2 (June 1998): 91–110.

Rogers, James G. *The Ste. Genevieve Artists' Colony and Summer School of Art, 1932–1941.* Ste. Genevieve: Foundation for Restoration, 1998.

Rosskam, Edwin, and Louise Rosskam. *Towboat River.* New York: Duell, Sloan, and Pearce, 1948.

Rozier, Firmin. *History of the Early Settlement of the Mississippi Valley.* St. Louis: G. A. Pierrot and Son, 1890.

Sagendorf, Bud. *Popeye: The First Fifty Years.* New York: Workman Publishing, 1979.

Sharp, Mary Rozier, and Louis J. Sharp. *Between the Gabouri: A History of Ferdinand Rozier and "Nearly" All His Descendants.* Authors, 1981.

Shrum, Edison. "Super Floods Raging in Wide Spread Area: *The Scott County Democrat*'s Account of the 1937 Mississippi River—New Madrid County Jadwin Floodway Disaster." Booklet. Scott City, MO; Author, January 1994, 1–3.

Sigafoos, Robert A. *Cotton Row to Beale Street: A Business History of Memphis.* Memphis, TN: Memphis State University Press, 1979.

Snider, Felix, and Earl Collins. *Cape Girardeau: Biography of a City.* Cape Girardeau: Ramfre Press, 1956.

Snow, Thad. *From Missouri: An American Farmer Looks Back.* Boston: Houghton-Mifflin, 1954. Reprint, Columbia: University of Missouri Press, 2012.

Stepenoff, Bonnie. *From French Community to Missouri Town: Ste. Genevieve in the Nineteenth Century.* Columbia: University of Missouri Press, 2006.

———. "The Last Tree Cut Down: The End of the Bootheel Frontier, 1880–1940." *Missouri Historical Review* 90, no. 1 (October 1995): 61–78.

———. *Thad Snow: A Life of Social Reform in the Missouri Bootheel.* Columbia: University of Missouri Press, 2003.

Stepenoff, Bonnie, Debbie Bibb, and Carla L. Jordan. "Three Mothers in Ste. Genevieve: Blending the Races, 1780–1890." *Gateway* 28 (2008): 44–55.

Strickland, Arvarh. "The Plight of the People in the Sharecroppers' Roadside Demonstration in Southeast Missouri." *Missouri Historical Review* 81, no. 4 (July 1987): 403–16.

Swift, James V. "From Pantry to Pen: The Saga of Commodore Rollingpin." *Missouri Historical Society Bulletin* 24, no. 2 (1968): 113–21.

Talbut, Mary Harriet. "The Bridge that Spanned the Great Depression." *Missouri Historical Review* 88, no. 2 (January 1994): 177–88.

Towey, Martin G. "Hooverville: St. Louis Had the Largest." *Gateway Heritage* 1 (Fall 1980): 2–11.

Twain, Mark. *Autobiography.* Vol. 1. Edited by Harriet Elinor Smith. Berkeley: University of California Press, 2010.

———. *Life on the Mississippi.* Mineola, NY: Dover, 2000.

Valencius, Conevery Bolton. *The Lost History of the New Madrid Earthquakes.* Chicago: University of Chicago Press, 2013.

White, William Robert. *Child of an Eagle: Mississippi Steamboating in Cape Girardeau, Missouri.* Cape Girardeau: Ramfre Press, 1980.

Williams, Dolores M. "Music on the Streckfus Steamers." *Bulletin of the Missouri Historical Society* 24, no. 3 (April 1968): 242–46.

Winther, Oscar. *The Transportation Frontier: Trans-Mississippi West, 1865–1890.* New York: Holt, Rinehart, and Winston, 1964.

Wright, Franklin. "Annie Cook: The Mary Magdalene of Memphis." *West Tennessee Historical Society Papers* 43 (1989): 44–54.

Index